sew fast sew easy
sew on

All You Need to Know to Start Sewing and Serging Today!

by
Elissa K. Meyrich

design and illustration
Dominic Harris

St. Martin's Griffin
New York

www.stmartins.com

Library of Congress Cataloging-in-Publication Data
available upon request

ISBN-13: 978-0-312-37892-9
ISBN-10: 0-312-37892-0

First Edition: June 2008

10 9 8 7 6 5 4 3 2

sew fast sew easy

sew on

Contents

Patterns are in the envelope at the back of the book.

Acknowledgements

I dedicate this book to my father who passed away at 93 while I was writing it. My roots are in the garment industry; my grandfather owned a textile company that my father worked for, that I walk by every day on my way in to the office of SewFastSewEasy on W 38th St.

I also want to thank all my students and customers as well as the patient teachers at SewFastSewEasy who teach my curriculum and keep me aware of how to make sewing fun and creative. I want to thank B.J. Berti — my steadfast editor, who has helped keep my goals to make an easy-to-understand book clear, and Dominic Harris for his special devotion to this book with his great skill and design sense. I also thank Gregory Garvin, Cara Peterson, Jordan Gant, Devon Nevola, Kerri Besse and Agata Chojnacka for constantly reminding me of how to inspire and teach a younger generation. As always I want to thank all the great patternmakers, drapers, and sewers I worked with during the wonderful years I worked as a designer in the garment industry. It was during this time that I really fine-tuned my professional skills and now am able to pass them on to the readers of this book. And last I always thank Mrs. Goldberg, my next-door neighbor, who when I was a child encouraged my curiosity about sewing, knitting, crocheting, and other crafts.

I am so grateful to the extra support Gregory Garvin gave me managing SewFastSewEasy while I was writing this book.

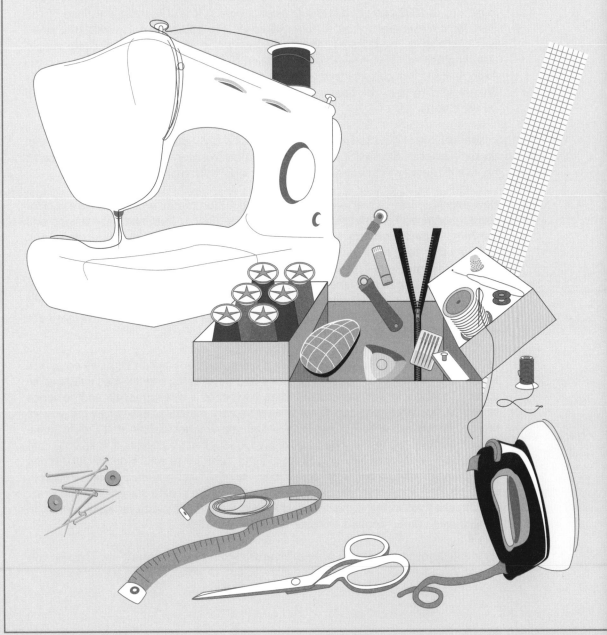

Do you ever find yourself saying; "I like it, but if only it had a little more flare." Or, "I want to be a designer or have my own boutique." The desire to make an idea come to life is what can get you started sewing it yourself. Welcome to *SEWFASTSEWEASY — SEW ON*.

My first book *SEWFASTSEWEASY — ALL YOU NEED TO KNOW WHEN YOU START TO SEW* came out in 2002 and set a trend in sewing books. It is still considered one of the best for new sewers today. It took a fresher, hip approach to sewing (the one I was teaching in my classes), as well as being one of the first to include simple sewing patterns. This new book expands on those methods (again drawing on my experience in my classes) to provide even more detailed directions and fabulous illustrations to help the beginning sewer or long time sewer needing to brush up on their skills.

I especially want guys to feel comfortable using this book; after all many men sign up for classes at SEWFASTSEWEASY, and this time we were able to include patterns for five projects which are designed to work for both men and women.

Now everyone loves to sew knits, so I have included learning to use an overlock or serger machine. This machine really opens the door to fast and easy sewing and finishing. Today's overlock machines are available at very affordable prices, and students that take my classes love to learn how to use it, especially when they see the quick, professional results they get. In this book you will learn how to thread and use an overlock machine and make a great fitting T-shirt and a sexy summer dress, how to sew leather, and how to sew cushions, as well as how to thread and use a regular sewing machine. All the techniques taught come from my garment industry skills and experience.

As I tell my students, "If you want to be a ballet dancer you can't just go *en pointe* the minute you want to. It takes practice and developing the muscles you need to do it." Sewing is a skill and a craft that also takes a little practice and patience to get the fundamentals down, but then it's just a matter of applying what you've learned to various different projects — and you will get better at it. You'll make lots of mistakes along the way. So have a good laugh at yourself and keep on going! That's how you learn. Not only does it build confidence and a delightful feeling of fulfilment when you finish something, sewing also makes you feel relaxed. Since you are using both your hands and your mind to create something, this craft also teaches you three-dimensional thinking, which helps with problem solving in general and can be applied to other areas of your life.

My greatest joy in life is being able to express myself through sewing and I hope it will be the same for you. I am continually curious and in wonder at the art of sewing.

ELISSA K. MEYRICH

Fabrics wrap around your life

CHECKLIST >>>

The most essential sewing supplies

1. Paper scissors

2. Fabric scissors

3. Clear ruler — to measure straight grain (2 x 18 inches long)

4. Tape measure — to measure body measurements and finished lengths

5. Dressmaker pins (size 17 or 20)

6. Tailor's marking chalk

7. Dressmaker's tracing wheel and tracing paper

8. All-purpose thread to match the fabric

9. Magnetic seam guide

10. Seam ripper

11. Sewing machine

With these tools and supplies you will be able to complete almost any sewing project or repair. You can find all the items in any sewing or craft store as well as from SewFastSewEasy.com

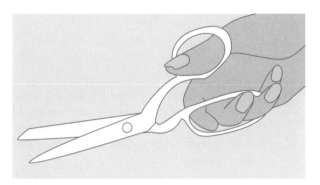

Scissors

You will need two pairs of scissors, one for paper to cut out your patterns, and fabric scissors for cutting out the garments. An 8-inch or 10-inch pair is my recommendation. The best kind is all metal. They will cut easily and last a long time. The fabric scissors become an extension of your hand and an extremely important tool.

The handles are designed for you to hold them a certain way to make cutting easier and more accurate. Insert the first three fingers of your hand into the longer oblong opening and your thumb into the circular opening.

Keep the scissors blades sharp; don't drop them, don't cut paper, salad, or any thing other than fabric with them, and don't let other people use them. Nothing is more frustrating than dull scissors.

Dressmaker pins

(size 17 or 20)
Pins come in all sizes and many varieties. Size 17 is the standard, but if you feel you might have trouble pinning then use size 20 since it's a little longer. Don't use dull or rusty pins—they will leave holes or marks in the fabric.

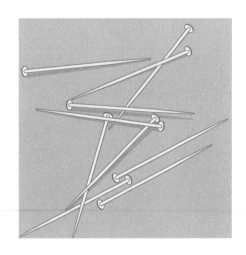

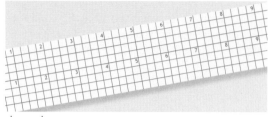

clear ruler

Clear ruler

(2 x 18 inches long)
A see-through ruler makes it easy to lay a pattern out correctly and mark corrections on a pattern or garment.

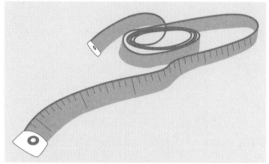

tape measure

Tape measure

A tape measure is important to have when measuring lengths, your body, width of fabric, etc. Some tape measures come with inches on one side and centimeters on the other.

tailor's chalk

Tailor's marking chalk, dry kind

Tailor's chalk comes in many forms: dry chalk, greasy chalk (like a crayon) and a powder in a dispenser. The dry chalk is the best to use and won't leave a grease mark.

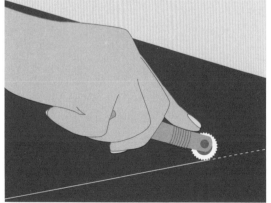

using a tracing wheel on tracing paper

Dressmaker's tracing wheel

Use with dressmaker's tracing paper, to transfer markings from the pattern to the fabric. Press down using a firm hand and move the wheel back and forth. Check to see if the marking is coming through onto the fabric.

Dressmaker's tracing paper

Use with the tracing wheel to transfer markings from the pattern or to draw new lines for alterations. Put the tracing paper in between or under the fabric in the area to be marked.

Magnetic seam guide

Use to guide the fabric through the machine evenly at the distance you want for seam allowance. With a ruler, measure the seam allowance from the needle position on the machine out toward the right on the needle plate, then line the magnet up with that measurement. Sewing straight seams is easy to achieve using the magnetic seam guide.

magnetic seam guide in position

Seam ripper

Even a good sewer can make a mistake. A seam ripper is used in two ways: to remove a few stitches or complete seams, use the point to lift and cut the loops of each stitch while pulling out the thread end; to remove larger areas, cut the thread in a few areas of the seam, then on the back of the fabric pull out the bobbin thread using the point of the seam ripper. It should be easy to pull away and is a quick way to remove unwanted stitches.

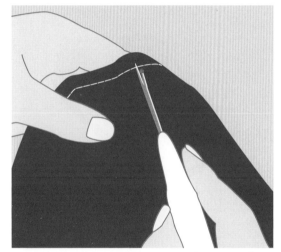

using a seam ripper

Thimble

It aids in pushing the needle through cloth when hand sewing and takes a little getting used to, but really helps your sewing technique. Choose a size that fits comfortably on your middle finger.

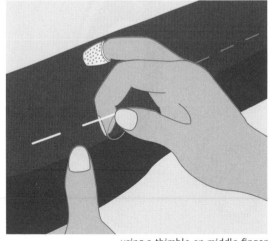

using a thimble on middle finger

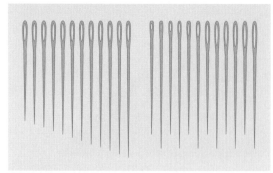

Handsewing needles

Use for hand-sewn hems, small repairs and embroidery. Use sharps or darners for sewing hems and repairs. Use tapestry needles when sewing through thick, stiff fabrics.

handsewing needles

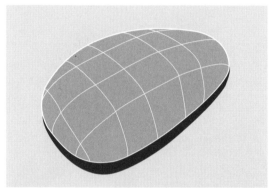

Tailor's or dressmaker's ham

A hard pillow, the plaid side is used for steam pressing shaped areas such as darts, sleeves, or curved areas. The other side of the ham is cotton and used for dry pressing. If you don't have an ironing board, this works as a replacement.

tailor's ham

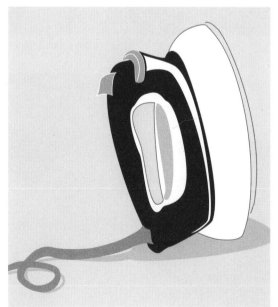

Steam iron

A good steam iron, that gives a lot of steam and has a heavy plate, makes pressing seams more effective.

steam iron

All-purpose sewing thread

When selecting thread for sewing garments and crafts, always choose all-purpose thread. There are many different types of threads meant for different purposes. For example, button and carpet thread is for sewing on buttons or repairing carpets; rayon thread is used for decorative machine stitching. Be careful not to buy the wrong kind, and don't ask for string or yarn when asking a shopkeeper where they are kept.

NOTE Always try to pick a thread color slightly darker than the predominant color or ground color of the fabric.

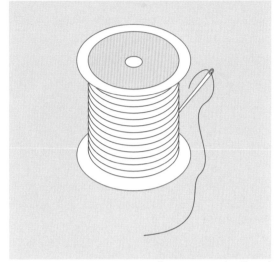

all-purpose sewing thread

Sewing machine needles

Keep a pack of assorted-size needles in your sewing machine in case you break a needle or two. Also, keep stretch knit needles on hand for sewing knits. Twin needles are useful for sewing a double needle finish like on jeans or knits.

sewing machine needles

A good sewing machine

There is nothing more frustrating than a sewing machine that does not work well. Make sure to clean the machine after sewing a few projects and change the needle. Use a compressed air can or small brushes, and refer to the manual that comes with the machine.

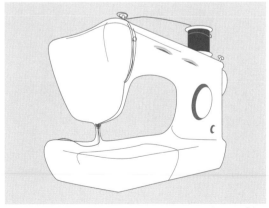

sewing machine

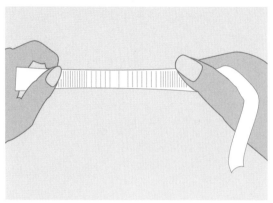

non-roll elastic

½-inch wide non-roll elastic

This is an all-purpose elastic used inside waistlines of pants and skirts. It will not twist around inside the casing of the garment.

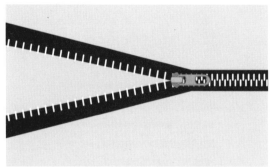

zipper

32-inch medium weight zipper

Zippers with metal teeth are best for heavy-use items such as cushions and blue jeans.

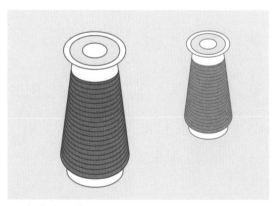

overlock thread

Overlock or serger thread

These are cones of thread designed especially for use on an overlock machine or serger.

Overlock machine or serger

This machine is a must when sewing a lot of knits. It is not necessary to buy a fancy machine with a lot of features. A good basic four-thread overlock machine will serve its purpose.

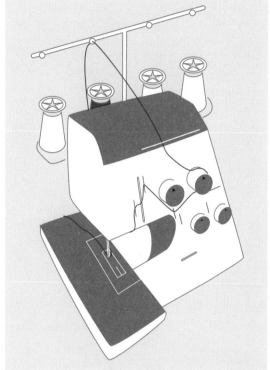

overlocker

Roller cutter and mat

This is an effective way to cut leather, suede, vinyl, and even strips of fabric. Use with a straight edge or ruler.

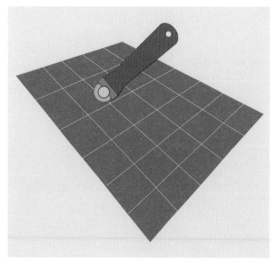

roller cutter and mat

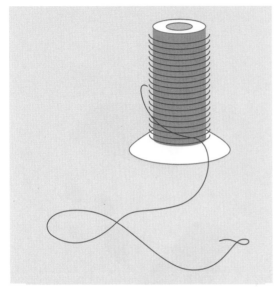

upholstery thread

100% polyester upholstery thread
Use for sewing leather or vinyl on a sewing machine.

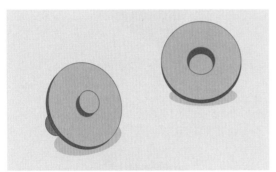

magnetic snap (male and female parts)

Magnetic snap
Use as a closure on accessories.

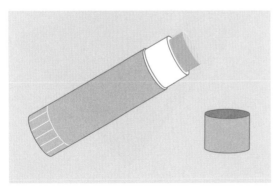

glue stick

Glue stick
Use to glue leather and lining fabric together, making it easier to sew.

What is fabric?

Fabric is a covering and is also called cloth or material. The oldest covering known to man is fur. Remove the fur and there is leather. Fabric is constructed by one of three methods — it can be woven, knitted, or non-woven.

Understanding the basics about fabrics

Did you know that 75% of the success of your sewing project depends on the fabric you choose? "It all starts with the fabric" as Francisco Costa, designer for Calvin Klein, says about his approach to design. A major fabric hunt goes on for most designers every season to find the right fabrics for each new collection.

Testing out different fabrics to decide on the best ones involves a lot of trial and error in the sample room of a designer. This can happen to you also. All in all, learning the best fabric to use is a process of trial and error until you gain a sense of it. This is especially true when you're a novice.

Do you know what you're wearing? Did you ever wonder whether the clothes you have on are made out of a knit or a woven fabric? It's very important to know that different fabric, depending on how it's constructed, can look, feel, and drape differently

Wovens These are constructed by interlacing the threads. The lengthwise threads or warp fibers are interlaced with the weft threads or horizontal running fibers. This process, known as weaving, creates woven fabrics that are produced on an industrial scale on large weaving looms.

Look at your jeans and you will notice that they are woven in a diagonal style called a twill weave. There are many other woven styles but plain weave, twill weave, and satin weave are the most common.

NOTE Denim is a particular woven fabric made from indigo dyed yarns developed from cotton fibers. The name denim comes from a town in France, De Nimes, where it first was woven.

Knits These are constructed by interlooping a length of yarn with each row dependent on the last. It looks somewhat like braiding. This process, known as knitting, is done using two knitting needles or with knitting machines.

Look closely at your T-shirt and you can see the loops that form the knit stitches. There are many styles of knits, such as jersey knits, double knits, and warp knits. A T-shirt is made from jersey.

Non-woven These are fabrics that are neither woven nor knitted but fused together. One of the oldest form of non-woven fabric is felt, and a modern high-tech one is Tyvek, which is commonly used for express mail (FedEx) envelopes. You can actually make a garment out of it.

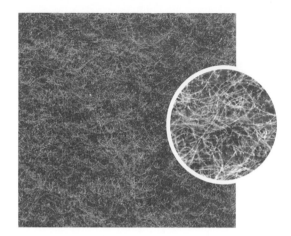

Leather This is made from animal skin after the fur is removed. There is also fake leather which is man-made.

Fur This is either the skin from an animal, or fake fur which is man made.

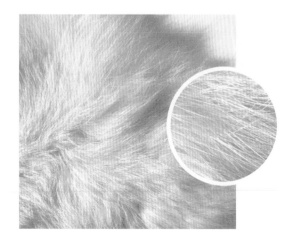

white border indicates selvage

band and fringes on the edge is selvage

selvage with small fringe and poke holes

The importance of straight grain

You might be unaware of the importance of finding the straight grain of your fabric but this step is crucial for making any garment hang properly when worn or even cushions that fit nicely. All pattern pieces are designed to follow the straight grain of the fabric and need to be cut properly, otherwise what you are making won't hang or fit well.

Finding the selvage

When fabrics are woven each side of the fabric is finished with an edge that looks like a band. This edge is called a selvage. The selvage runs along the length of the fabric on both sides. Look carefully at the fabric you bought, you will be able to identify the selvage by looking for this:

Does it have little holes poked into it? Does it have a little fringe running along either side? Or does it have a woven or printed band running along either side?

Finding the selvage on knits

You can usually identify the selvage on knits by finding the band of glue blotches or fine poke holes along the edges of the fabric.

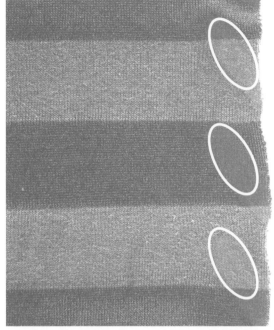

glue blotches

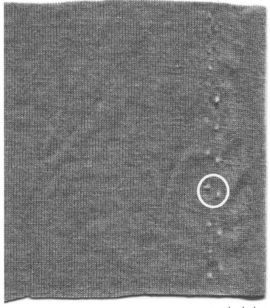

poke holes

Warp

By locating the selvages you have also found the lengthwise straight grain of the fabric, which is also called the warp in textile terminology. The warp threads are the strongest threads in the weave of a fabric. That is why most garments are cut to hang with the warp of the fabric running vertically on your body. It allows the garment to hold its shape.

Weft

A textile term meaning the cross grain of the fabric. The weft threads run back and forth horizontally from selvage to selvage. The weft has a little give and is softer than the warp.

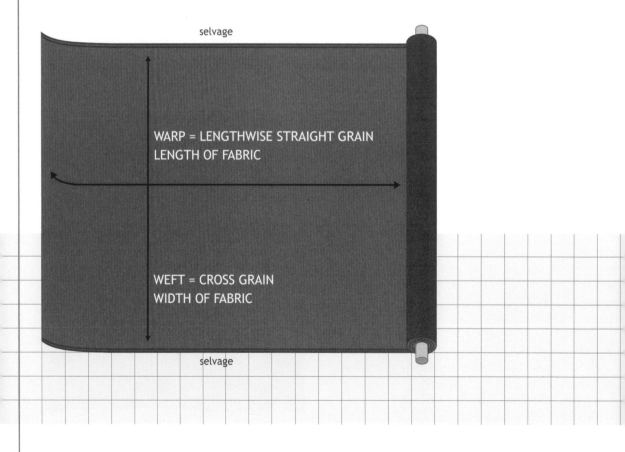

selvage

WARP = LENGTHWISE STRAIGHT GRAIN
LENGTH OF FABRIC

WEFT = CROSS GRAIN
WIDTH OF FABRIC

selvage

Bias

This is a term used to describe any diagonal line across the fabric. True bias is at a 45-degree angle to the fabric's straight grain. Garments cut on the bias hug the body and take the shape of its contours. The fabric hangs soft and drapey. This diagonal line also gives fabric its greatest point of stretch. Bias cut garments use more fabric yardage and therefore are more expensive.

Designers use true bias to create sexy evening gowns like ones worn at the Oscars. You can also use a bias cut strip of fabric to make a neckline and armhole finish, soft bows, or piping for trim.

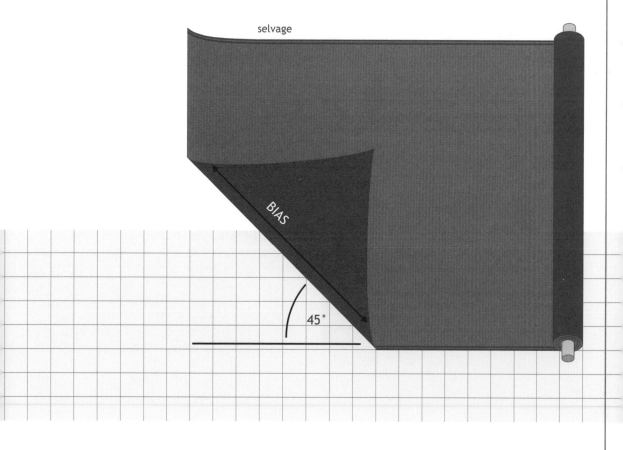

selvage

BIAS

45°

woven satin dress with a printed face that takes up the whole front of the dress

What are fibers?

Fibers are natural or man-made filaments that are spun into individual strands of yarn that are either woven or knitted to make fabric. Fabrics today are often a blend of natural and synthetic fibers, for example the blends of cotton and Lycra used in T-shirts and workout clothes, or the polyester and wool blends used in suits.

Fibers play an important role in the fabric's performance. For example there are smart fabrics that are designed to resist stains, or workout clothes to help you swim faster. Today's manufacturers and designers are looking for fabrics that are made of eco-friendly fibers such as soy, bamboo, and hemp. Fiber made from soy has the look and feel of cashmere when knitted into sweaters.

Fashion from hippy to hip

There is an amazing advancement in the technology of new fabrics. Today's textiles are merging with elements of art, engineering, and science. Some designers, having realized the importance of the fabrics they choose to work with, are creating textiles themselves. Others work with textile designers to conceive something unique for their collections.

How to look at fabric

- If you are attracted to a fabric — hold it in your hand and identify if it is woven or knitted by looking along the cut edge across the width. If the raw edges are frayed then it is woven; if the raw edges curl slightly then it is knitted.
- Examine the fabric carefully for interlacing or interlooping yarns. Use a magnifying glass if necessary to help you identify a knit or a woven fabric.
- Hold a yard of the fabric close to your body. Drape the fabric over your leg for a pant; for a skirt hold the fabric so it hangs from your waist down; and for a top, hold it close to your torso. Look down at it and imagine it in the garment you are planning to sew. If there is a mirror in the store do this in front of a mirror. If you have someone with you ask him or her what he or she thinks.

How to buy it

- Fabric is sold by the yard and rolled off a bolt or tube. Fabric is woven in several widths. The most popular widths are 52 to 54 inches and 58 to 60 inches wide. Often you can find very fine woven cottons that are 44 to 45 inches wide. Rarely, some fabrics are 32 to 35 inches in width.
- Leather, suede, and fur are sold by the square foot. Some, such as lambskin and suede, are soft and lightweight, making them easier to sew.
- A safe amount of fabric to buy if you are not sure of how much you need is 3 yards.
- Contrary to the old-fashioned belief that fabrics should be washed before they are sewn, this is not true. Modern store-bought fabrics have been finished and are prepared to be cut into garments. If you decide to wash any cottons, rayon, knits, or silks they should never be dried in a dryer. Heat will make any fabric shrink. The only time it pays to prewash a fabric is if you are dyeing it or you want to soften it or give it a special effect.
- Go right ahead and be spontaneous. Turn the music up and dive right in by cutting and sewing when you get the urge to be creative.

Best fabrics for the projects in this book

When you're a novice at sewing or you haven't sewn for a long time, it's best to start out with a fabric that won't give you a hard time when cutting and sewing. Fabrics have personality too. For example if your impulse is to buy a drapey silk charmeuse for the drawstring pants in chapter 7, be prepared for a tough customer since charmeuse swooshes around, which makes it a challenge to cut and sew. On the first page of each project is a list of the best fabrics to use for each.

The patterns

For the projects in this book you will NOT have to buy a commercial pattern. They all are in the envelope on the inside back cover of this book. Open the envelope and take the pattern tissues out, working on a table or other flat surface. Carefully open up the folded patterns and you will find that you have five patterns in total:

1. Drawstring pants
2. T-shirt
3. Scarf halter wrap-around dress
4. iPod holder
5. Box cushion and ottoman cover

Pattern layouts

All patterns come with a layout and instructions on how to sew the garment. But another way to save time is by following either of the two basic layouts below. Once you get used to cutting and sewing several projects, these general layouts can be used for cutting out almost all patterns. The illustration shows that pants can be cut by folding the fabric lengthwise or widthwise as long as the fabric is folded selvage on top of selvage.

In chapter 8 (T-shirt), a different layout is used for cotton and lycra knit in order to avoid the crease line in these fabrics. Sometimes these knits have a permanent crease in them that will not come out in the wash. You wouldn't want that line in the front or back of your T shirt.

Sewing pattern terms

All sewing patterns have symbols that mean something. Here are the symbols to look for on a pattern and what they mean.

Straight grain line

This symbol means that the pattern should be placed parallel to the selvage of the fabric. Always use a ruler to make sure that the pattern piece is equidistant from the selvage of the fabric at each end of the straight grain line.

Fold line

This symbol means the pattern should be pinned to the fold line of the fabric and opened after it is cut. You do NOT cut along the fold line.

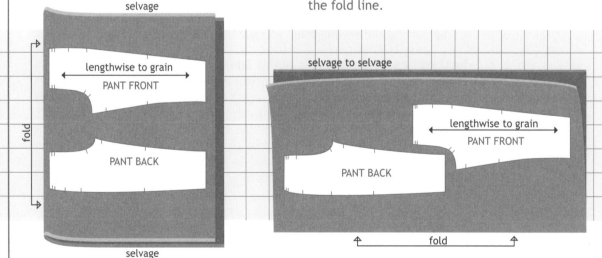

Notches

These symbols indicate matching points to other pattern pieces. They are very important in helping assemble the garment correctly. After cutting out the pattern piece, but before unpinning it, check to see that the fabric has been clipped for notches. Using the tips of the scissors, clip only ¼ inch into the triangle.

DO NOT cut out the triangle; it's time consuming and will weaken the fabric.

Notches can be indicated by either triangles or a line.

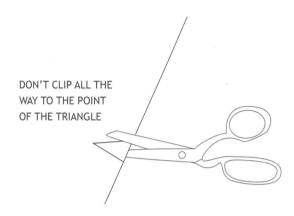

DON'T CLIP ALL THE WAY TO THE POINT OF THE TRIANGLE

Cutting lines

Patterns have different cutting lines to identify the different sizes. They can be solid lines, broken lines or dashes. Make sure to cut on the line that matches or comes the closest to your measurements. All patterns have a little extra ease in each size for comfort and movement on your body. If in doubt use a size that is slightly bigger as you can always take in but you can't add on.

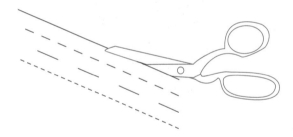

Seam allowance

A pattern term meaning the distance between the cutting line and the sewing line of a pattern. Most of the patterns that come with this book have ½ inch seam allowance that is garment industry standard. All American commercial patterns have a ⅝ inch seam allowance in their patterns unless otherwise noted.

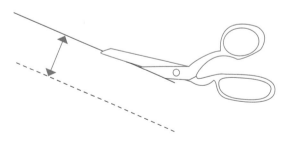

Before choosing a pattern size to cut, first take the measurements needed in order to determine the size that will fit best.

For the drawstring pants you will need the hip measurement.

For the T-shirt you will need the bust or chest measurement.

For the scarf halter wrap-around dress you will need the bust measurement.

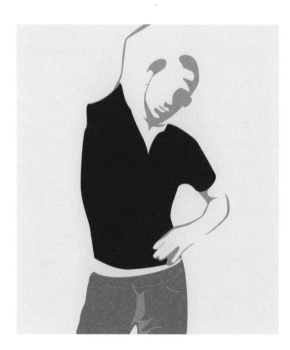

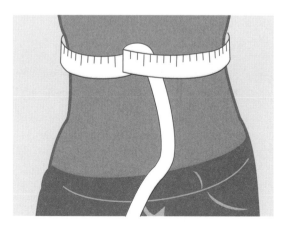

In order to create a garment using the patterns in this book or any commercial pattern you must know how to correctly take your body measurements. You cannot go by the sizing used for clothes that are bought in a store, catalog or online. Patterns are not sized like store- bought garments. You must first take your measurements and then use the size chart provided on page 127 to determine which size pattern to cut out or buy.

Here's how to take your measurements
In order to find your hip measurement, first find your TRUE waistline. The hip measurement is the most important measurement for selecting the correct size pattern to use for making pants and skirts.

Waist
Find your true waistline by tilting your body to the side as if you were exercising and doing a side tilt. Put your right hand on your hip and your left hand up over your shoulder, creating an arc. Start bending toward the right. You will feel your body form a crease on the right-hand side. Repeat on your left side. The creases are your waistline. Wrap the tape measure around your waistline and measure your waist, making sure the tape measure is comfortable and not too tight. Record this measurement.

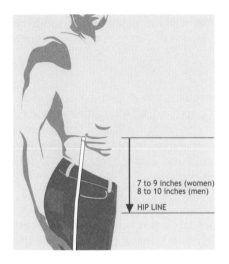

7 to 9 inches (women)
8 to 10 inches (men)

▼ HIP LINE

Bust and chest

For women, wrap the tape measure around your shoulder blades and across the fullest point of your bust. Be careful to keep the tape at an even height. Don't let it slide down your back. Use a mirror to check that it's even. For men, measure your chest by raising your arms slightly and measuring just under your arms. Be sure to cross over the shoulder blades and the fullest part of the chest.

Hip

Finding your hip is much easier once you've found your waist. Tie a length of string or elastic around your true waist. Now take the tape measure and place the end on your waistline letting it drop to the floor. For women your hip line area can be anywhere from 7 to 9 inches down from the waistline. For men it's 8 to 10 inches down from the waistline. Use your eye to guide you around the fullest area in the 7 to 10 inch range. Once you have found your hip line area wrap the tape measure around this area, being very careful not to let it slip down, especially around your backside. Record this measurement making sure the tape is resting evenly around your hip line and not pulled too tight.

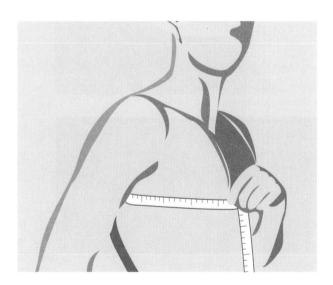

All of the garment patterns in this book require using the size chart on page 127. If you are using commercial patterns, they also have a size chart, printed on the envelope. This has other information including all notions and yardage needed for each style shown.

Now you're ready to cut out the patterns and lay them onto the fabric.

If you follow these rules you will be able to cut all garments out efficiently and quickly. This method of cutting and laying out patterns is used professionally in the garment industry. It will ensure sewing success on any project you make.

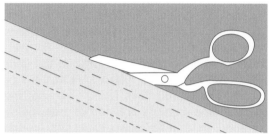

cut on the line indicated for pattern size

press out your fabric

folding fabric: selvage to selvage

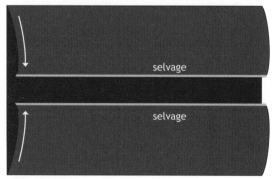

folding jersey fabric for T-shirt project

Rule 1

Determine the correct pattern size and cut out the pattern following lines indicated for each size using the paper scissors. Not all projects have multiple sizes. The iPod holder and the cushion/ottoman in this book are one size.

Rule 2

Press your fabric if it is very wrinkled. Press your pattern if it is very creased. For the pattern use a dry iron (no steam), since it is made of paper or tissue.

Rule 3

The right side of the fabric is called the face. Always fold the face inward so that it is on the inside of the folded fabric. The exception to rule 3: when folding velvet the face goes on the outside.

Rule 4

When folding the fabric, make sure the edges are placed evenly together, selvage on top of selvage. Take time to smooth out your fabric so there are no ripples, and it is lying flat on the table.

The exception to rule 4: when using a jersey knit fold the selvages or side edges of the fabric in toward the middle of the fabric instead. Measure the folded-in sections so they are even in width from the folded edge to the selvage. This method of folding the fabric will insure that the crease usually found in knits does not land on the center front or center back of the T-shirt.

Some jersey knits are finished with a permanent crease line in the middle of the fabric. This crease line will never wash out.

Rule 5

Pin down all of the pattern pieces following the straight grain line or the fold line, as marked, on the pattern. Follow the pattern layout in each chapter. When using a commercial pattern follow the layout on the instruction sheet that comes with the pattern.

Rule 6

Make sure the arrow on the pattern piece marked "straight grain line" is absolutely parallel to the selvage of the fabric or fold line. Use a ruler to measure from the straight grain line on the pattern to the selvage or fold of the fabric. The measurement should be the same at each end of the straight grain line. Pin the grain line down before pinning the rest of the pattern piece. Don't overpin the pattern. Only a few pins are needed.

Rule 7

Cut out the pattern pieces as smoothly as possible with the scissors. If you cut evenly, you will be able to sew your project together much more easily. Take small snips, using the tips of the scissors. Keep your eye on the pattern line.

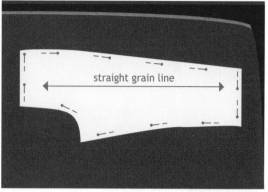

pin following the straight grain line

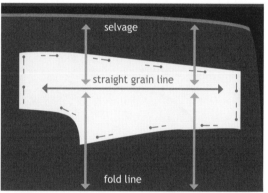

make sure the arrow on pattern pieces are parallel to the fold line or selvage

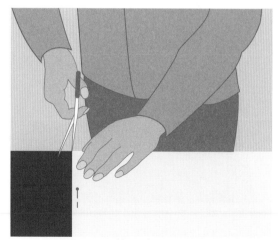

cutting smoothly with scissors, using small snips

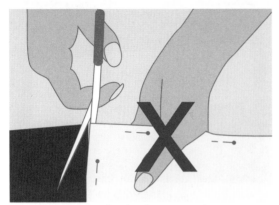

never slide your hand under the pattern pieces

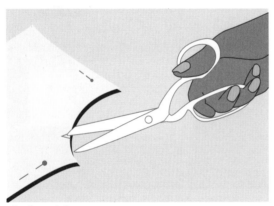

clip the notches

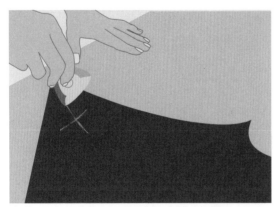

chalk mark an "X" on wrong side of fabric

Rule 8

When you are cutting, never move the pattern pieces that are pinned to the fabric and never slide your hand under the pattern pieces.

Rule 9

Clip the notches on the pattern pieces using only the tips of your scissors. Do not cut out the triangle, just clip into the center of the triangle.

Rule 10

Before you unpin the pattern pieces, mark an "X" with tailor's chalk on the wrong side of the fabric on each pattern piece. This is a very helpful way to identify the wrong side of the piece if the fabric looks identical on both sides.

NOTE ON SLIPPERY FABRICS

If you have slippery fabric such as silk or chiffon, make sure to run the selvage of the fabric along a table that has a straight edge. This helps to keep the fabric lying on a perfect grain. In addition you can tear the fabric at the very top to find the even (weft) cross grain.

Then when you lay it on a table and run the length of the fabric along the length of the table, the top of the fabric (where you tore it) should be even too. The fabric will be on a perfect straight grain if it forms a right angle lying on the table.

In addition to this method, it is always easier done if you first lay down a layer of paper and then lay the fabric on top of the paper. Recommended paper is dotted pattern paper or tissue paper. The paper grips the slippery fabric which makes it easier to layout the patterns and cut out the pieces.

CHECKLIST >>>

When laying out and cutting patterns:

(1) Determine the correct pattern size and cut on line for the size.

(2) Press fabric if wrinkled and press pattern with dry iron if creased.

(3) Fold the face or right side of fabric inward, except when using velvet.

(4) Lay fabric out evenly and smooth out any wrinkles. If folding, place selvage on top of selvage.

(5) Pin the pattern pieces following the pattern layout and pattern symbols.

(6) Make sure the arrow on the pattern piece marked "straight grain line" is pinned parallel to the selvage or fold line.

(7) Cut pattern pieces evenly.

(8) Don't move pinned pieces while cutting them out.

(9) Clip all the notches with the tips of your scissors.

(10) Chalk mark an "X" to indicate the wrong side of the fabric and then unpin the pattern pieces.

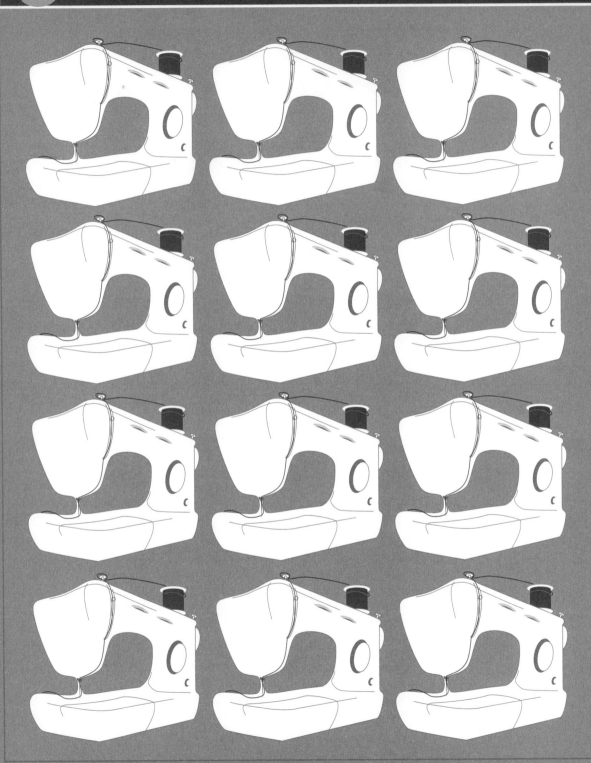

A sewing machine is an appliance. It is the only household appliance that works with gears and a belt, a lot like a motorcycle or a car. However, it remains in a stationary position.

Like any appliance, start by plugging it in and turning it on. All sewing machines work the same way and they thread in a similar way too. Once you've learned how to use a sewing machine you can use any make of sewing machine. They all follow a similar threading pattern that has not changed much since the time of their invention.

> **NOTE** The first sewing machine was invented by Elias Howe in 1846, then produced for the mass-market in 1850, when Isaac Singer built the first commercially successful sewing machine.

A sewing machine creates a lock stitch. For example, these are the little stitches you see on the collars and pockets of a shirt.

A sewing machine is threaded from the bottom of the machine with a bobbin and from the top of the machine with a spool of thread. Always use the all-purpose thread that is sold on small spools designed to fit on a home sewing machine. Cones of overlock thread, button and carpet thread, or industrial cones of thread do not work well on home sewing machines.

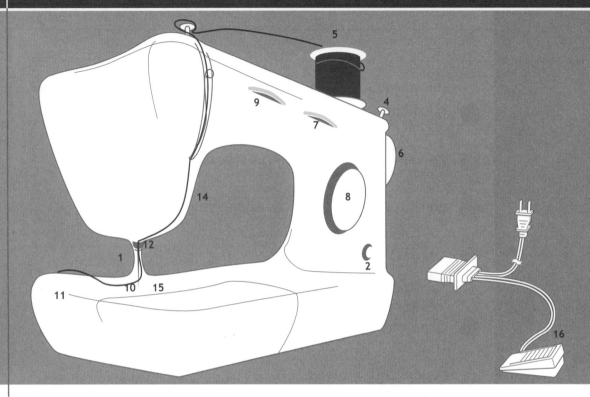

Needle [1] Threads from front to back on most of today's machines. Needles come in different sizes and types for sewing different kinds of fabrics. Always use the right needle for the fabric that is being sewn. (Refer to needle chart on page 127).

Reverse button [2] Used for finishing off and locking the stitches so they won't open up. Called back tacking or back tack.

Bobbin and bobbin case [3] A small plastic or metal spool that holds the bottom or lower stitching thread. The bobbin sits in the bobbin case which is inserted into the machine under the needle plate.

Bobbin winder [4] Winds thread onto an empty bobbin. Usually on the top of the machine next to the spool pin holder. Most machine models automatically stop the

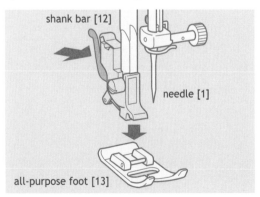

shank bar [12]

needle [1]

all-purpose foot [13]

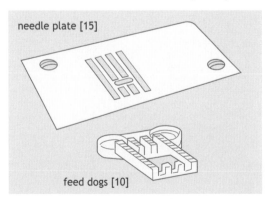

needle plate [15]

feed dogs [10]

needle from moving up and down while you wind a bobbin, but on some machines you have to turn a stop-motion knob, which is located on the outer rim of the hand wheel.

Spool pin holder [5] Located on the top of a machine. Some are vertical and some are horizontal. If horizontal, it has a spool-cap cover to keep the thread from flying off while sewing or winding the bobbin. Some machines have two spool pin holders so you can sew with two spools of thread at the same time while using twin needles.

Handwheel [6] Turns manually to make the needle go up and down. Always turn the handwheel toward you.

Stitch length dial [7] Makes the stitch longer or shorter. Better models also have a dial for stitch width to make the stitch wider or narrower.

Stitch pattern dial [8] Most machines have various functional and decorative stitches as well as a buttonhole stitch.

Thread tension dial [9] Controls the tension flow of the top thread.

Feed dogs [10] The feeder mechanism that pulls the fabric through the machine while it is sewing. You do not have to pull or push the fabric while sewing. The machine will do this.

Free arm [11] Allows you to sew small areas that are hard to get to, like cuffs on a shirt. To use, remove the accessory tray, which is attached along the side of the free arm.

Shank bar [12] Where the shank adapter screws on in order to attach sewing feet. Most machines today are low shank, while older machines can be high shank. It is important to know whether your machine is low or high shank when you buy new feet for your machine.

All-purpose foot [13] All machines come with this attached to the shank bar. There are many feet you can buy to make your sewing easier and more professional looking. There are feet for different finishes or for use as sewing guides. For example, a Teflon foot will make sewing on leather or plastic much easier.

Presser foot lifter [14] Located either on the back or the side of the machine, this handle lifts the presser foot up and down. Also it lifts up a little higher in order to put thicker fabric under the presser foot.

Needle plate [15] The metal plate over the feed dogs and where the needle goes down to pick up the bobbin thread.

Foot controller with power cable [16] Use this to control the sewing speed. Never put your foot on the controller while threading the machine.

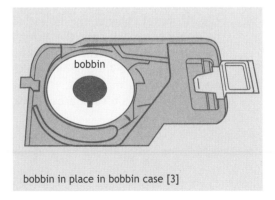

bobbin in place in bobbin case [3]

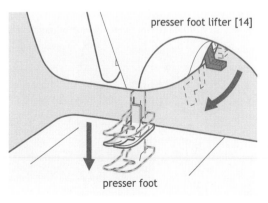

presser foot lifter [14]

presser foot

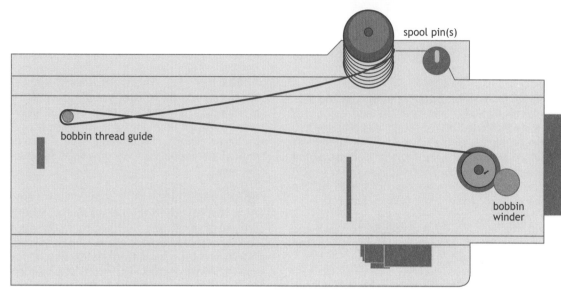

steps 1.1–1.2 (view from above)

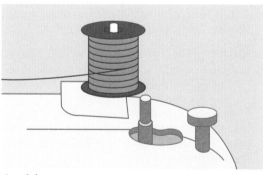

step 1.1

steps 1.2–1.5

1. Winding the bobbin

1.1 Place your spool of thread on the spool pin. Don't forget to put the spool carrier cover onto the thread if it is on a horizontal spool pin. Some machines have threading diagrams pasted onto the machine.

1.2 Take the thread from your spool, pull it around the bobbin thread guide, and then thread it through the center hole (if metal, one of the holes) of the bobbin, making sure the thread is going out through the top of the bobbin hole. Place the bobbin on the winder. On some machines, you only have to wrap the thread around the bobbin.

1.3 Always push the bobbin winder toward the right. Disengage the clutch if the machine has one (usually on the handwheel).

1.4 Press gently with your foot on the controller to wind the bobbin.

1.5 While doing this, check to make sure the thread is winding on the bobbin tightly and not below the bobbin winder. When you are done, push the bobbin winder to the left, back into sewing position.

1.6 Cut the bobbin thread after winding the bobbin.

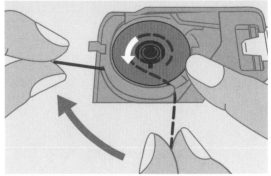
step 2.1

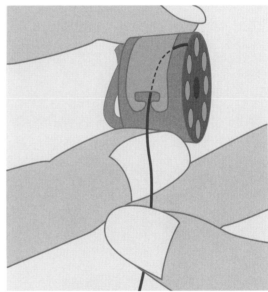
step 2.2

2. Loading the bobbin into machine

2.1 If you have a top-loading machine (drop-in bobbin), you drop the bobbin into the case already in the machine. Make sure the thread is properly pulled into the slit for tension.

2.2 On a side-loading machine (oscillating bobbin), place the bobbin into the removable bobbin case, making sure the thread is properly pulled into the slit for tension.

2.3 Insert the bobbin case into the compartment on the side of the machine and close the cover.

2.4 Refer to your machine's manual for bobbin winding and loading.

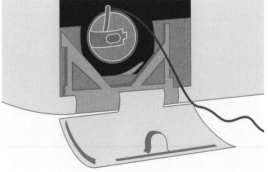
step 2.3

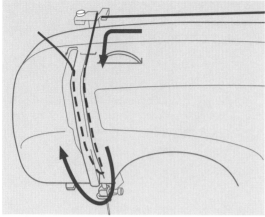

step 3.1 — threading direction

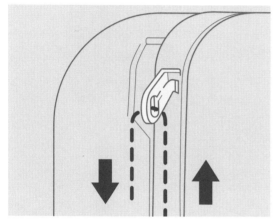

step 3.1 — take-up lever

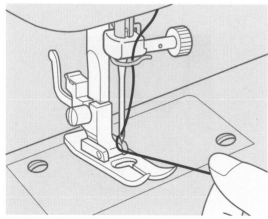

step 3.2 — threading the needle

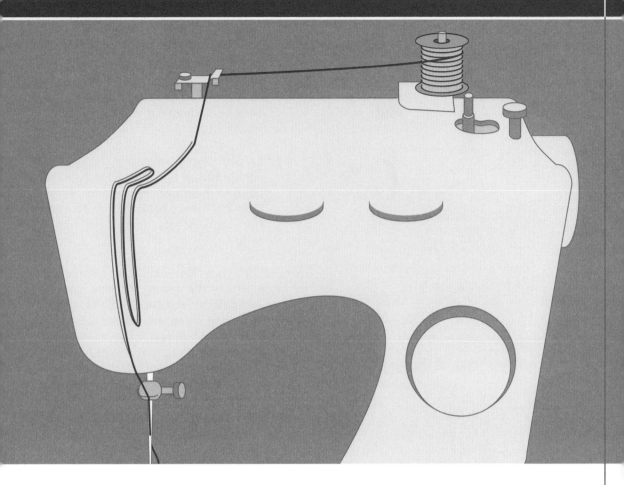

3. Threading the top of the machine

3.1 Thread the machine by going through the thread guides, then through the tension discs to the u-turn and up to the take-up lever, making sure the thread is IN the eye of the take-up-lever, then pull down into the remaining thread guide(s) and thread the needle.

3.2 Generally, you thread the needle from front to back.

EXPERT TIP If you can't see the eye of the needle, place a small white piece of paper behind it in order to refract the light.

3.3 Check to make sure you have threaded the machine properly. Remember, in order for the thread to be in tension, it must be pulled through the tension discs inside the machine (which you don't see), so when threading into the u-turn and up through the take-up lever, give the thread a tug.

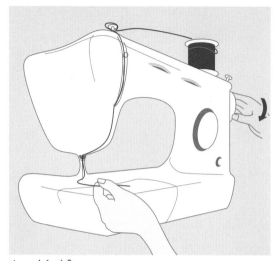

steps 4.1–4.3

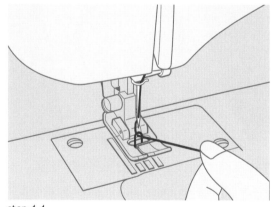

step 4.4

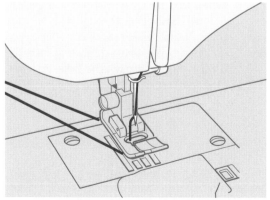

step 4.5

4. Just before sewing

4.1 Make sure to leave 6 inches of thread coming through the needle so it doesn't become unthreaded when you begin to sew.

4.2 Before sewing, you must bring the bobbin thread up through the needle plate to the top of the machine. With your left hand, hold the top thread from the needle loosely in front of you.

4.3 With your right hand, turn the hand-wheel of the sewing machine slowly TOWARD you until the needle has gone down and made only one rotation.

4.4 As you are doing this, keep holding the top thread from the needle with your left hand until you see a loop on it. That is the bobbin thread. Then take your two fingers and pull the bobbin thread out toward you.

4.5 Place both the needle and bobbin threads under the presser foot and toward the back of the machine.

You now have threaded the machine and you are ready to sew.

CHECKLIST >>>

Before you sew

1 Plug the sewing machine in and turn it on.

2 Thread the machine correctly. Refer to the instruction book that comes with the machine.

3 Always keep your foot off the foot control while threading the machine.

4 Check to make sure the stitch length is between 2.5 and 3 and the pattern selector is on the straight stitch.

5 Are the threads from the machine placed under the presser foot toward the back of the machine?

6 Is your fabric placed under the presser foot a little past the needle of the machine?

7 Is your presser foot lever down?

8 Make a back tack by sewing a few stitches forward and backward, then forward again to lock the seam.

9 Sew slowly — don't "floor-it"!
Don't pull the fabric through the machine — the feed dogs will move the fabric as the machine is sewing.

lock stitch

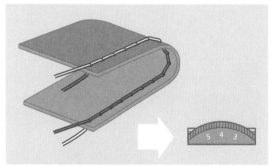

correct tension — don't move dial

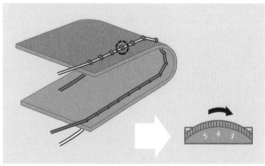

loose top tension — turn dial up

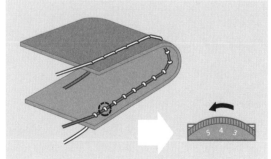

loose bottom tension — turn dial down

The stitch

All sewing machines create a lock stitch. The needle goes down inside the machine and creates a lock stitch by looping with the bobbin thread. This is one rotation. After several rotations on a piece of fabric it will form a continuous straight stitch. This holds the two pieces of fabric together.

Thread tension

The tension of the thread is very important and affects the quality of the machine's stitches. The tension on a machine is usually set, but if thicker fabric is used or a special effect is desired then the tension might need to be adjusted.

Trouble shooting tips

If the machine is creating loops for stitches, then check to see if it has been threaded properly. Most of the time improper threading is the problem. If the stitches are still too loose, then determine if it is the top thread tension or the bobbin tension that is loose. If it is the top tension then turn the tension dial up a number. If it is the bobbin thread then adjust the flow of the thread by turning the screw on the bobbin case. If the fabric is puckering then loosen the tension.

Also check the needle to see if it is bent or dull. Replace with a new needle in the size that is suitable for the fabric you are using. (Refer to needle chart page 127).

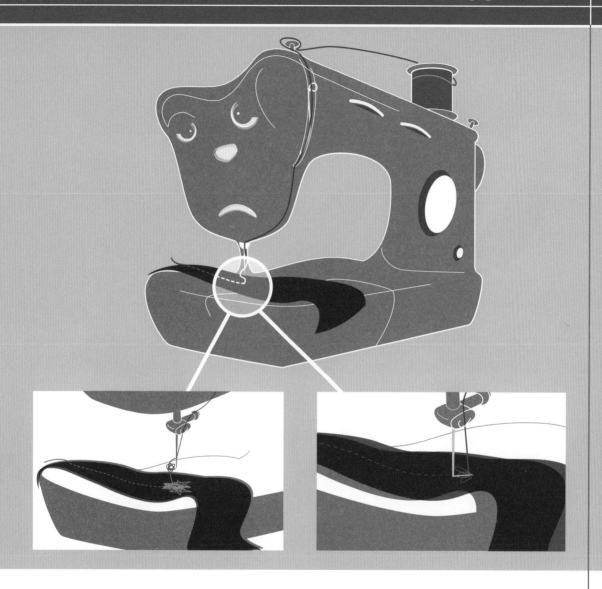

Sewing machines can jam

All sewing machines, no matter how expensive, can jam for various reasons. The most common reasons are improper threading and the fabric not feeding properly through the machine because it's too thick. If your machine jams up, DON'T pull the fabric out! Carefully cut the threads away to release it. Pulling will throw the machine's hook timing off, then only a repairman can fix it.

Breaking needles

Without warning the needle can break; sometimes the needle is too thin for the thickness of the fabric you're sewing, or it is slightly bent from use, or you are pulling and not letting the fabric feed on its own through the feed dogs of the machine. Changing needles after at least one or two projects will help.

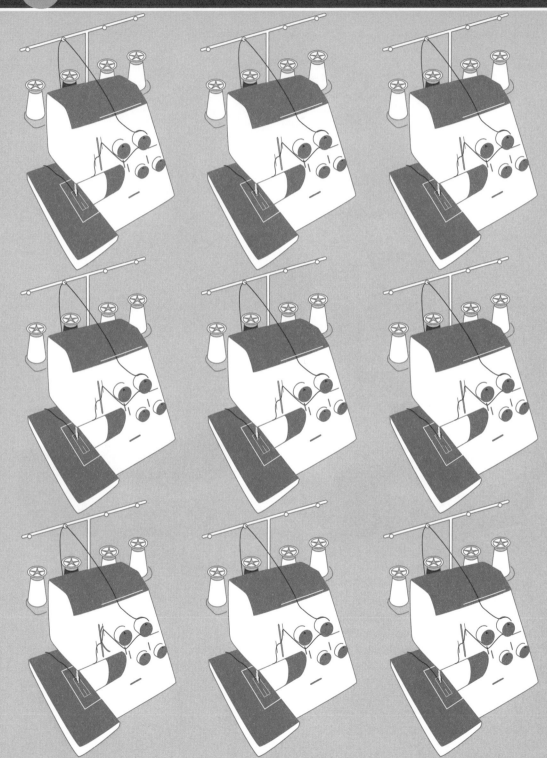

An overlock machine for home use is also an appliance like the sewing machine. Start by plugging it in and turning it on. These machines are also called sergers, because some of them do more than overlock stitching. A true serger is a five-thread overlock machine that sews a safety stitch chain as well as an overlock stitch, all at the same time.

All overlock or serger machines sew by using loopers and needles to create an overlock stitch. Therefore it does not have a bobbin. An overlock machine will both sew and cut the edges of fabric to finish off seams so they won't fray during washing or wearing. This stitch can be seen on the inside of all mass-produced garments. An overlock machine is threaded by using four cones of overlock thread designed for use on these machines. Do not use all-purpose sewing thread; buy only cones of overlock or serger thread.

Overlock machines are extremely versatile and are especially efficient for sewing knitted items and swimsuits, finishing scarf edges, and finishing edges of cut seams while reinforcing them at the same time.

An overlock machine does not replace a sewing machine. It can't sew a buttonhole or a zipper in place, can't top stitch, and can be awkward on sharp curves. However, it will save hours of time, especially on knits.

NOTE Overlock stitching, also commonly known in the garment industry as "merrowing," was invented by the Merrow Machine Company in 1881. The Merrow company developed this machine to sew knits. Over time, the Merrow Machine Company pioneered the design of new machines to create a variety of overlock stitches, such as a rolled-hem, also known as a pearl edge stitch in the garment industry, a serge stitch with a safety chain, and a cover hem stitch.

Spool pin holders [1] These are used to hold the four cones of overlock thread. They stand on a thread stand in the back of the machine.

Thread tension dials [2] These set the balance of the tension. Unlike sewing machines, the overlock machine has four tensions to adjust: one for each thread in use. The stitches are formed by tightening or loosening the tensions, as well as by using one or two needles to sew with. Some machines have automatic and/or self-adjusting tension settings. Sometimes these settings need to be adjusted to get the overlock stitch to form correctly.

Thread guides [3] On top and inside the front of the machine are thread guides that must be followed in order to thread an overlocker properly. Generally there is a threading chart to follow on the inside cover of the machine.

Loopers Loopers create thread loops by looping around the threads from the needle and onto the edges of the fabric. The overlock stitch forms over the edge of one or two pieces of cloth to make edging or a seam while at the same time trimming the fabric edge.

Upper looper [4] The upper looper interacts with the lower looper to create the overlock stitch. The upper looper thread should always be threaded before the lower looper thread. Follow the threading chart in the instruction book or on the inside cover of the machine.

Lower looper [5] The lower looper generally has a thread guide on it that must be threaded first and then the thread passes through the tiny hole on the end point of the looper. When threading, the lower looper thread should then pass over the top of the upper looper.

Needles [6] A machine uses two needles to make a standard overlock stitch. If both needles are used the stitch is a true overlock

stitch, used for sewing knits and wovens as well as finishing off raw seams. When using only one needle and disengaging the stitch finger, the stitch forms a rolled-hem, also called a pearl edge stitch. This stitch is an excellent finish for a scarf or the neckline of a T-shirt. A three-thread stitch, also using one needle but leaving the stitch finger in place, forms a narrow seam finish that looks better on silks, satins, and fabrics where a narrow finish is preferred.

Stitch length adjuster This feature adjusts the distance between stitches. Sometimes you have to open the side cover to get to it, and on other machines it's found on the outside of the machine.

Upper knife blade [7] There is an upper and lower blade on an overlock machine. It trims the fabric while the machine is making the overlock stitch. It can be moved or adjusted when necessary. Follow the instructions that come with the machine.

Presser foot [8] It snaps on and off like a sewing machine foot.

Presser foot lifter This is a small handle located on the side or back of the machine used to lift the presser foot. When you begin to sew there is no need to lift the foot as on a sewing machine. Just feed the fabric into the machine and the differential feeds move the fabric through.

Differential feeds [9] On a sewing machine they are called feed dogs. On an overlock machine they do the same thing. However, on an overlock machine, the differential feeds affect the look of the stitch. They also affect whether the finished edge is flat or wavy. When set to neutral, the two layers of fabric will feed equally and smoothly. They can also be adjusted to gather one layer on top of the other. For a decorative finish, set the differential to gather fabric into a ruffled look that is called lettuce edging.

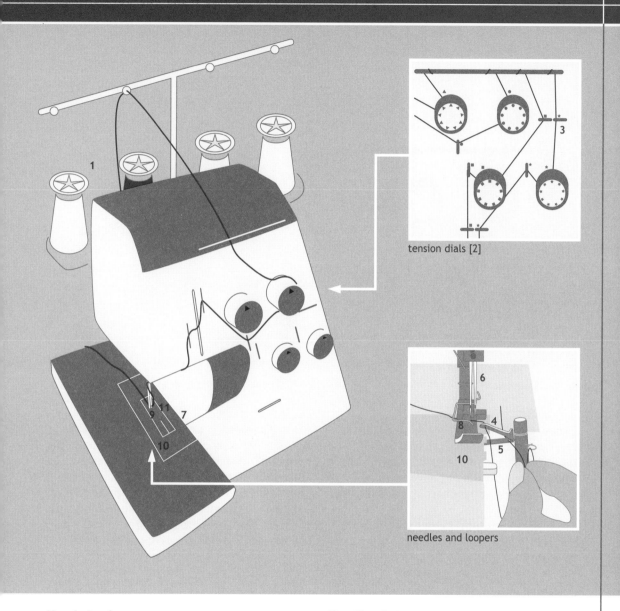

tension dials [2]

needles and loopers

Handwheel Like on a sewing machine, it turns manually and makes the needles go up and down. Remember, always turn the handwheel toward you.

Foot controller with power cable
This controls the sewing speed. Never put your foot on the controller while threading the machine.

Needle plate [10] This is the metal plate cover that has the opening for the teeth of the differential feed.

Stitch finger [11] This is the small metal piece on the right side of the needle plate. The threads from the needles and the loopers wrap around the stitch finger and form an overlock stitch. It can be disengaged to make a smaller stitch.

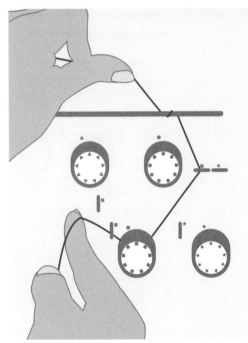

fig. 1 — tension dials

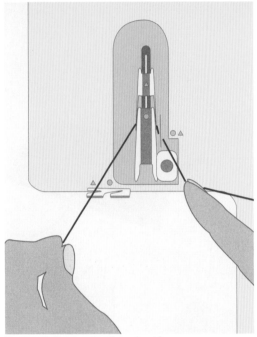

fig. 2 — following the thread guides

Cones of thread are placed on spool pin holders, which are located in the back of the machine. They are then threaded into a telescopic spool stand that is color coded to match the threading chart on the machine.

Keep the tweezers that come with the machine and a sharp scissors handy to cut the thread.

EXPERT TIP

Cut the thread, moisten the tip with your lips, and it will thread easily through the looper holes and the needles. Use the tweezers also.

Here's where your attention is needed!
When wrapping the thread around the thread tension dials, pull the thread in an upward motion, making sure it is really in the tension dial (fig. 1). Pick up the presser foot by raising the lifter when doing this. This is very important in order to make sure your stitches don't look loose and loopy.

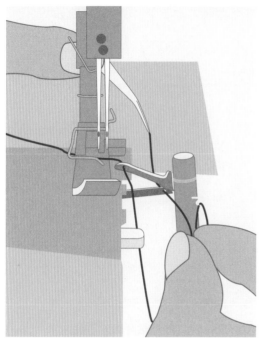

fig. 3 — upper and lower loopers

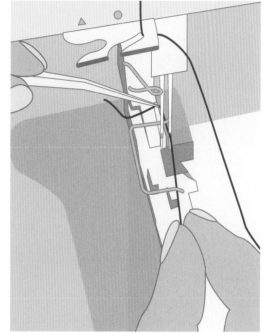

fig. 4 — threading right needle

An overlock machine threads from right to the left (facing the machine) and must be done in the following order:

1. First thread the **upper looper** (fig. 3), following the thread chart on the inside cover of the machine. Thread very carefully and make sure to pull the thread through the hole on the tip end of the looper. Take the remaining thread and extend it under the presser foot toward the left.

2. Next thread the **lower looper** (fig. 3), again following the thread chart. The lower looper has a thread guide on the back end of the looper that must be threaded. Check to make sure your thread is going through all the thread guides (fig. 2) and in the hole on the tip of the looper.

EXPERT TIP

The lower looper thread should always be carried over and on top of the upper looper. Then bring the remaining thread under the presser foot toward the left of the machine.

3. First thread the **right needle** (fig. 4) by carefully following the threading chart and making sure to pull the thread up into the tension dial and all the thread guides. Thread the needle from front to back and bring the remaining thread under the presser foot toward the left of the machine.

4. Next thread the **left needle** by following the threading chart and repeating step 3.

5. Double check to see that you didn't miss a thread guide, tension dial, or the loopers, otherwise the threads will break and not form a lock stitch.

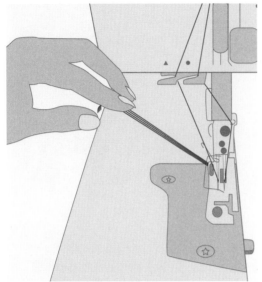

fig. 5 — hold the threads at the back

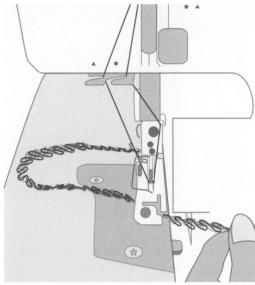

fig. 7 — cutting off the stitches after sewing

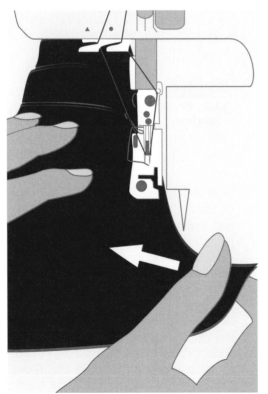

fig. 6 — direction to move fabric when sewing curves

Starting the overlock machine

Start the machine by pressing lightly with your foot on the foot control. The machine will begin forming an overlock stitch. At the same time, use one hand to hold back the beginning threads at the back of the machine (fig. 5).

When sewing around curves always gradually move the fabric away from the cutter following the edge of the curve. Go slowly and look at the fabric as it goes through the machine (fig. 6).

Finishing off

While running the overlock machine, use your fingers to bring the overlock stitches around to the front of the presser foot and cut them off by using the motion of the blade (fig. 7).

CHECKLIST >>>

Before you sew

1. Always plug the overlock machine in and turn it on.

2. Check to make sure all four threads are wrapped around the tension dials as well as through the thread guides.

3. Check if the threads are through the holes on the tips of the loopers and eyes of the needles.

4. Always keep your foot off the foot controller while threading.

5. Make sure approximately 8 inches of all four threads extend under the presser foot and are going toward the left of the machine.

6. Make sure the presser foot is down.

7. Turn the handwheel towards you by hand two or three times to get the stitch started.

8. Test drive the machine using a scrap of knit fabric. Remember not to lift the presser foot. Use your finger to pick up the front of the presser foot just a bit and slide the fabric under the tip of the foot.

9. NO-NOs — Don't pull the fabric! Don't stretch the fabric! You will bend or break the needles or cause the stitches to break.

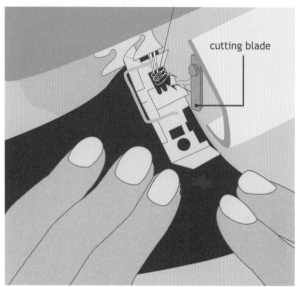

cutting blade

avoid cutting your fingers

BE CAREFUL!
Since an overlock machine has a cutting blade, be careful where you put your fingers while guiding the fabric through the front of the machine.

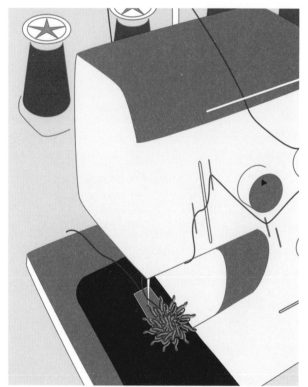

an overlock machine can jam

Like a sewing machine, an overlock machine can jam.

Keep your eye on the blade and the looper to make sure the fabric is being cut and sewn properly and nothing is getting stuck on the stitch finger or the loopers.

If the machine jams, stop sewing and cut the threads to clear the fabric.

Make sure to remove any pins in fabric while feeding it into an overlocker.

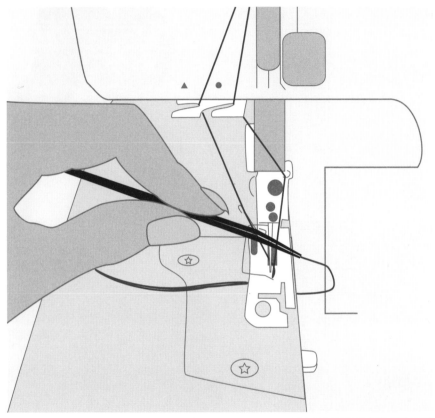

use tweezers to help rethread

Broken threads

If the threads break, cut them and pull them out of the machine.

Make sure the threads from the needle are not wrapped around the lower looper. If they are, slide them off the looper with tweezers and rethread.

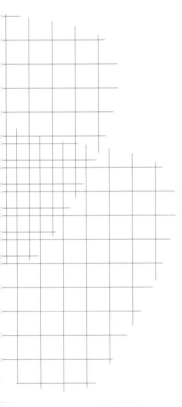

What you need to make them

Materials
3 yards of fabric for all sizes, 45 or 60 inches wide
2 squares of light-weight fusible, 1½ x 1½ inches wide
1 yard of non-roll elastic, ¾ inch wide
All-purpose thread to match fabric

Fabric suggestions
Soft cotton, silk, rayon, linen, or any lightweight
stretch woven or knit fabric.

Don't buy heavy or stiff fabrics or fabric with a printed
or embroidered border running along the selvage.
Don't use swimwear fabric or panne velvet.

Tools
Paper scissors
Fabric scissors
Dressmaker pins (size 17 or 20)
Clear ruler (2 x 18 inches long)
Tailor's chalk
Dressmaker's tracing wheel and tracing paper
Sewing machine
Magnetic seam guide
Seam ripper
Iron and ironing board

> **NOTE** This drawstring pants pattern fits both male and female.
> Make sure to measure your hip and check size chart on page 127.

Skills you will learn
How to sew a pair of pants with on-seam pockets
How to make an elastic drawstring with ties
How to make a casing
How to make buttonholes

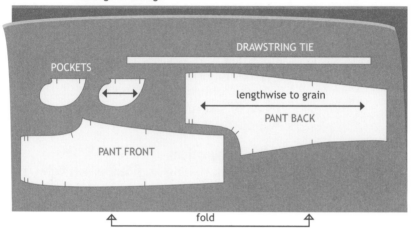

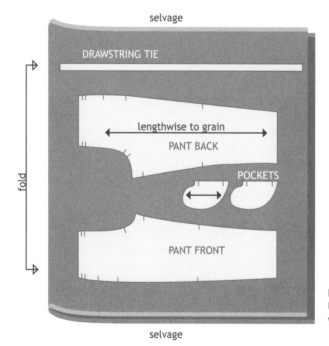

selvage to selvage

DRAWSTRING TIE

POCKETS

lengthwise to grain

PANT BACK

PANT FRONT

Layout A
Use for 60 inch
wide fabric

fold

selvage

DRAWSTRING TIE

lengthwise to grain

PANT BACK

fold

POCKETS

PANT FRONT

Layout B
Use for 45 inch
wide fabric

selvage

1. Cutting Instructions

Cut out the pattern pieces and pin the pattern to the fabric following the layout (A or B).

Cut: 2 pant fronts
2 pant backs
4 pockets
1 drawstring tie

2. Checklist of notches to clip

Pant front: 1 crotch, 2 side seam pocket, 2 inseam, 1 side seam, 4 casing
Pant back: 2 crotch, 2 side seam pocket, 2 inseam, 1 side seam, 4 casing
Pockets: 2 side seam

Clip all your notches using the tips of your scissors.

3. Before starting to sew

3.1 Chalk mark an "X" on all pattern pieces to indicate the wrong side of the fabric.

3.2 Unpin the back leg pattern and lay the two cut pieces faceup.

3.3 Unpin the front leg pattern and lay the two cut pieces facedown on top of the back pieces.

step 3.1

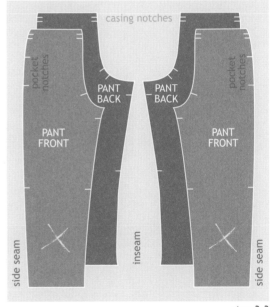

step 3.3

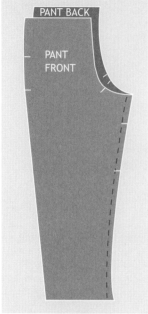

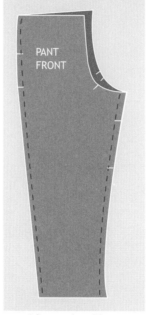

step 4.2 — sewing inseam on one leg

step 4.3 — sewing side seam on one leg

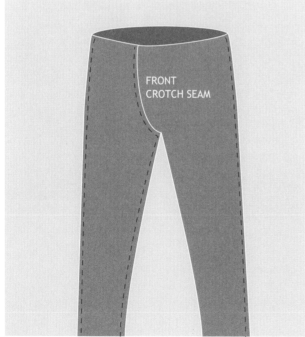

FRONT CROTCH SEAM

step 4.4 — sewing crotch seam

4. Joining pant leg inseams and side seams

4.1 Pin the inseam backs to inseam fronts. Pin the side seam backs to side seam fronts.

4.2 Sew the inseams together using a $1/2$ inch seam allowance.

4.3 Sew the side seams together using a $1/2$ inch seam allowance.

> NOTE Don't sew over your pins.

> EXPERT TIP
> Use a magnetic seam guide on your machine. Then you will be able to sew straight and even seams.

4.4 Join the two pant legs together by sewing the crotch seam. Pin the crotch seam starting at the center front, matching the front crotch notches and the inseams at the curve of the crotch, and continue around to the back, matching the center back notches. Continue until you get to the center back waist. Now that you have the crotch line pinned, sew it together using a $1/2$ inch seam allowance.

5. Fitting your drawstring pants

5.1 When your pants are sewn together, try them on. You might want a more tapered fit in the legs, or you may want to adjust the crotch if it is too low or too tight. You may also want to lower the pants to even a lower hipster fit.

5.2 Pin a piece of elastic around your waist where you like to wear your pants. For example, if wearing hipster style, place the elastic so that it rests on the low hip area. Pull up your pants and adjust them so that they are comfortable. Slip them under the elastic.

5.3 Make sure your pants are centered on the front and back of your body and the side seams are on the sides of your legs. When making fitting adjustments, it is only necessary to fit one leg and then transfer the pin marks to the other leg. If you have a lot of extra fabric at the top of your pants, fold the fabric over your elastic and pin it just below the elastic. Mark the pins with chalk. You only have to chalk mark one side of your pant from center front to center back.

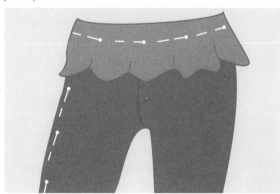

step 5.3

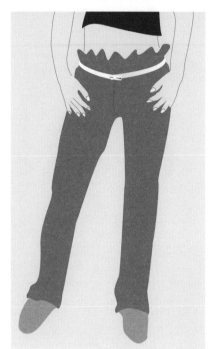

step 5.2

6. Tapering your pant leg and adjusting the fit

6.1 If you want to taper the pant leg, look at your pants in the mirror and place pins along the side of the leg marking the taper line. At your waist, check if you have too much excess fabric on the side creating extra fullness that you might want to remove. If so, unpin the elastic and using both hands at your waistline side seams, pinch in the sides and start to pull the pants down over your hips.

6.2 Can you pull them down easily? Can you take out some of the excess at the side seams? If so, pin out this excess and test if you can pull your pants down over your hips. If not, loosen the pinned excess.

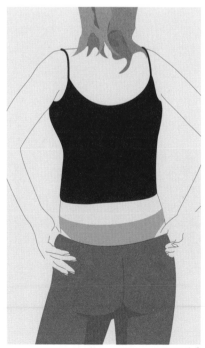

step 6.2

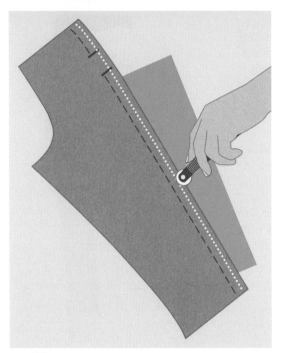

step 7.3

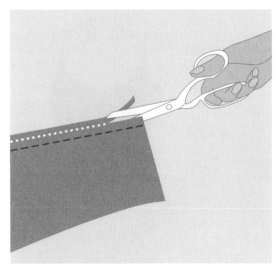

step 7.4

7. Marking your pinned corrections

7.1 Step out of your pants and lay them on a table. Turn pants inside out so the wrong side is facing out. Take marking chalk and carefully rub a mark where the pins are in pants. Now remove the pins.

7.2 The chalk marks are the new taper line. With chalk and ruler connect the marks to create a smooth line. This will be the new stitching line. Fold the pant exactly in half so that one pant leg is on top of the other

7.3 Using a tracing wheel and tracing paper, mark the new stitching line onto the other side of your pant.

7.4 Stitch on new lines then try pants on again to check the fit. If fine, cut away the excess leaving a $1/2$ inch seam allowance from your sewing line.

8. Sewing on-seam pockets

8.1 After you've completed the above steps, open the side seams from the top to 3 inches below the bottom of the pocket notch. With right sides facing, pin pockets to pant fronts and backs matching the notches at the side seams to the pocket notches.

8.2 Sew pockets to side seams of pants using a $1/2$ inch seam allowance on all four pieces. Turn pants to wrong side and press pocket seams open flat. Pin together the open side seams of the pants. Chalk mark the pocket opening starting $3^{1}/2$ inches down from the top. The pocket opening should be $5^{1}/2$ to 6 inches long. Then chalk mark the end of the pocket opening.

8.3 Sew the side seam opening together starting at the top of the pant using a $\frac{1}{2}$ inch seam allowance. Stop at the top chalk mark opening. Machine back tack. Then skip the pocket opening and continue down the side seam of the pant until you close the remaining side seam opening. Do this on both sides.

8.4 Sew the pockets around the outside edges starting at the seam allowance of the pant pocket opening and ending at the top of the lower pocket opening. Machine back tack.

NOTE If you don't want pockets, join the side seams starting from the top of the pant and continue to sew to the bottom of the legs using a $\frac{1}{2}$ inch seam allowance.

9. Making the elastic drawstring with ties

9.1 Measure your waist from side seam to side seam across your back using a tape measure. Cut elastic to that measurement.

9.2 Fold the drawstring tie in half and cut to make two ties.

9.3 Prepare the two ties for sewing by pressing them in half lengthwise. Then fold in the $\frac{1}{2}$ inch seam allowances toward the wrong side and press again. You can do all of this at the ironing board.

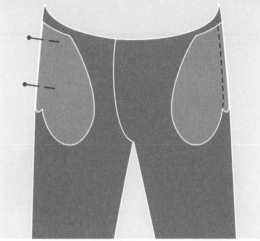

steps 8.1–8.3

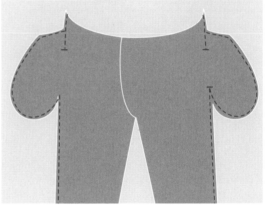

step 8.4

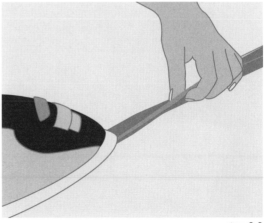

step 9.3

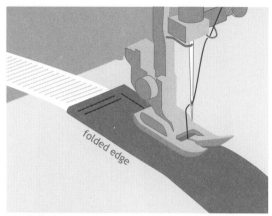

step 9.5

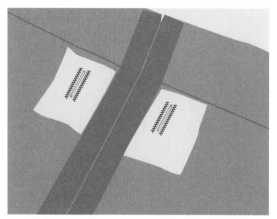

step 10.3

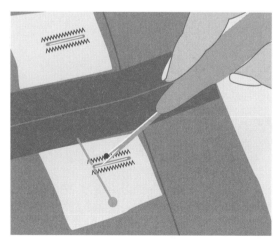

step 10.4

9.4 Next, pin the fabric ties onto each end of the elastic.

9.5 Sew a top stitch on the ends of the fabric ties securing the elastic and along the open edges you just pressed. Use an edge stitch that is $\frac{1}{8}$ inch from the edge. Set aside.

10. Make buttonholes for drawstring

10.1 On the right side mark two vertical buttonholes on the center front of the pants, one on each side of the center front seam. Follow the buttonhole marks on the pant pattern.

10.2 On the wrong side of the pants, iron two $1\frac{1}{2}$ inch squares of fusible onto the marked buttonhole placements. This will keep the buttonholes from stretching.

10.3 Make two buttonholes following your sewing machine instruction manual.

10.4 Carefully cut open the buttonhole with a seam ripper. Before cutting open, place a pin at the end of the hole so you won't cut past the threads while opening it.

11. Make casing for drawstring

11.1 Use either a zigzag stitch on the sewing machine or an overlock machine to finish off the raw edge at the top before making the casing for the drawstring. It is also a good time to finish off all seams on the pants as above if desired.

11.2 Measure down from the top of the pants $1\frac{1}{4}$ inch, then bend in to the wrong side. Press flat, making sure you have made a sharp crease line. This will become the casing for the elastic drawstring.

12. Insert drawstring and sew casing

12.1 Insert drawstring under pressed top edge close to crease line. Pull ties through the buttonholes to the front side of pants and knot ends together so you don't loose drawstring in the casing.

12.2 Change to a zipper foot on the sewing machine. Starting at the front, close to the buttonholes, machine stitch 1 inch down from the top of the pant to form casing for drawstring. Use a magnetic seam guide or chalk mark 1 inch for the stitching line.

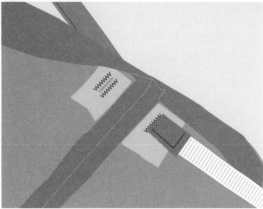

step 12.1

13. Hemming pant legs

13.1 With your pants on, bend over and put a pin to mark where the pant hits the arch of your foot. This is a good standard length for pants.

13.2 Fold the pants flat on a table, with one leg on top of the other and the inseams of both pant legs meeting.

13.3 Turn the excess fabric below your pin mark up onto the leg of the pant. Make sure both legs are the same. It is easy to do this with one leg on top of the other.

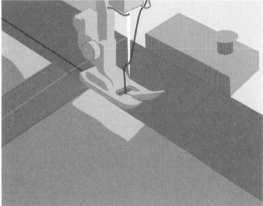

step 12.2

13.4 Try on your pants before trimming away excess. Trim away any excess leaving 1¼ inches for the hem. Turn the raw edge under ¼ inch and pin the hem in place.

13.5 Press and sew at the edge of the hem on the wrong side of the pant legs.

Your pants are now ready to wear.

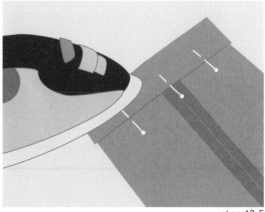

step 12.5

What you need to make it

Materials
1 $^1/_2$ yards of fabric for all sizes, 60 inches wide
All-purpose thread to match fabric
4 spools of overlock/serger thread to match fabric

Fabric suggestions
Lightweight jersey knit fabric, 100% cotton, or a blended fabric like cotton and Lycra, or rayon and Lycra.

Don't use swimwear fabrics.

Tools
Paper scissors
Fabric scissors
Dressmaker pins (size 17 or 20)
Clear ruler (2 x 18 inches long)
Tailor's chalk
Sewing machine
Overlock machine or serger
Twin needle suitable for knits

NOTE This T-shirt pattern fits both male and female. Make sure to measure your bust or chest and check the size chart on page 127.

Skills you will learn
How to mark and cut knits
How to use an overlock machine or serger
How to set in sleeves using an overlock machine or serger
How to make a professional finish on the neckline of a T-shirt
How to use a twin needle to make a professional hem finish

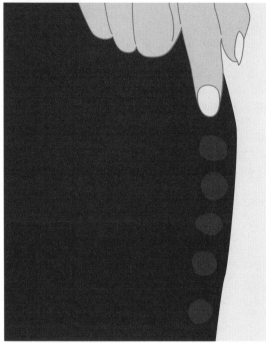

identifying glue spots

Laying out patterns on knit fabric

- To start, identify the selvages by looking for the finished glue spots running down the lengths of each side of the fabric.

- Fold each of the selvages in toward the middle with the right sides of the fabric folded in. Make sure the folded section is even so the fabric is lying on the straight grain.

- Measure the folded section, making sure this measurement is consistent all the way down the length of the fabric on both sides. Smooth out the wrinkles if there are any. The fabric should be lying completely flat.

fold selvages in toward middle of fabric

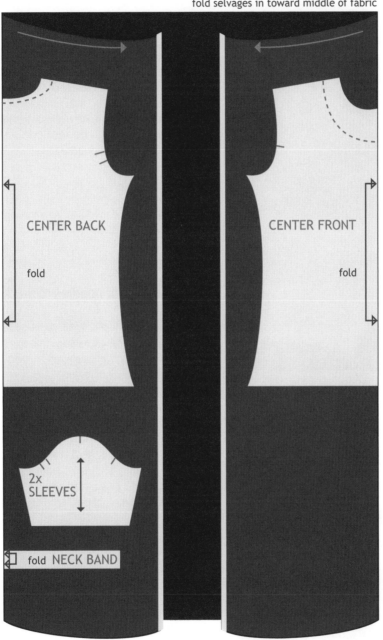

male neckline

female neckline

CENTER BACK

fold

CENTER FRONT

DO NOT CUT
ALONG FOLD

fold

2x
SLEEVES

fold NECK BAND

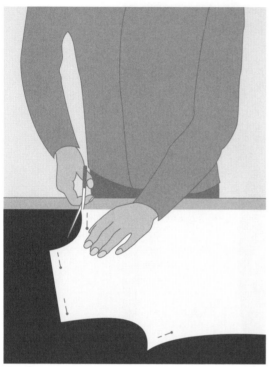

step 1

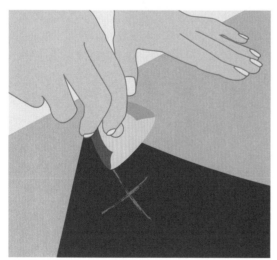

step 3.1

1. Cutting instructions

> NOTE Before cutting out your size be aware that the neckline on the pattern is different for men's and women's T-shirts.

Cut out the pattern pieces and pin the pattern to the fabric following the layout on page 71.

Cut: 1 front
      1 back
      2 sleeves
      1 neckband

2. Checklist of notches to mark

> NOTE For knits it is best to chalk mark notches, not clip them. You will see the notches more easily when overlocking the seams.

Front: 1 front armhole on each side, 1 center front neckline (on fold line)
Back: 2 back armholes on each side, 1 center back neckline (on fold line)
Sleeves: 1 shoulder point, 1 front armhole, 2 back armholes
Neckband: 1 center front (on fold line)

> NOTE Make a chalk mark at center front and center back. Fold at neckline before unfolding cut pieces.

3. Before starting to sew

3.1 Chalk mark an "X" on all pattern pieces to indicate wrong side of fabric.

3.2 Unpin the back pattern, open, and lay the cut piece faceup. Unpin the front pattern, open, and lay the cut piece facedown on top of the back piece.

3.3 Pin the shoulder seams together and get ready to use the overlock machine.

> **CAUTION** Always place the pins so they are not actually pinned on the shoulder seam but approximately 1 inch away to insure that they do not get caught in the overlock blade.

3.4 Using some scraps of your knitted fabric, do a test run through the overlock machine to make sure it's threaded correctly and the stitch setting is good for the fabric you are using. Practice running fabric through the overlock machine as per instructions in the overlock basics chapter.

4. Assembling the T-shirt

4.1 Overlock the shoulder seams together.

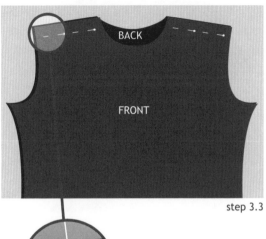

step 3.3

step 3.3 detail

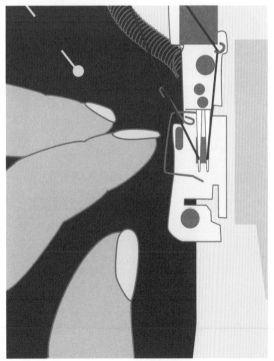

step 4.1

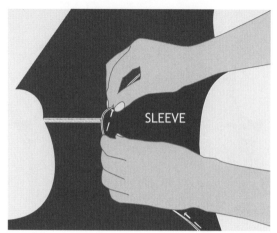

step 4.2

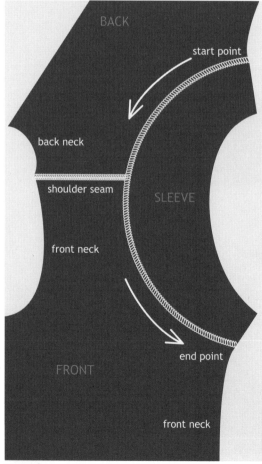

step 4.3

4.2 Next, pin the sleeves into the armholes with right sides facing, making sure to match the shoulder point notch on the sleeve to the shoulder seam line of the T-shirt, and the notches on the front and back sleeve to armhole notches.

4.3 Starting at one end of the armhole, overlock the armhole seams together, ending at the other end of the armhole.

> NOTE If you've never sewn an armhole or a curve using an overlock machine, cut out a curved piece the shape of an armhole on a leftover piece of fabric and practice overlocking.

4.4 Pin the side seams and underarm seams together, making sure the pins are at least 1 inch away from the side seam, and making sure to match the front and back armhole seams together. Start sewing from the bottom edge of the T-shirt, finishing at the end of the sleeve.

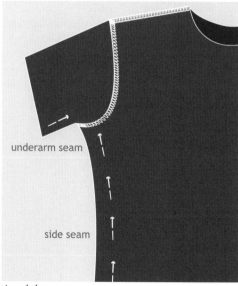

step 4.4

In order to always get a nice fit at the neckline of the T-shirt:
The stretch on the neckband piece should be 2 inches smaller than the neckline of the T-shirt. Even though the pattern piece for the neckline is made to fit the neckline of the front and back pattern, it is always wise to test the knit you are using for the T-shirt to make sure the band has just the right fit. If it is too relaxed or too tight it won't look good.

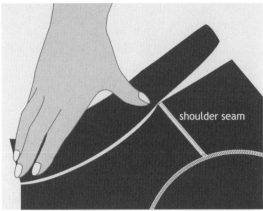

shoulder seam

step 5.3

5.   Making the neckband fit

5.1   You will have to do this for every type of knit fabric you buy.

5.2   Fold the cut neckband in half and chalk mark on the fold; then fold the neck opening of the T-shirt in half so that there is half of the front, shoulder seam and back neck showing.

5.3   Take the center front of the neckband and match it to the center front of the T-shirt and slightly stretch it with your fingers around toward the shoulder seam.

5.4   Chalk mark the neckband at the stretched out point, where it meets the shoulder seam. Keep stretching the band a little and continue around to the center back and chalk mark this point on the band.

5.5   Leaving a $^1/_2$ inch for seam allowance, cut off the excess from the neckband if there is any.

5.6   The neckband may sometimes be difficult to handle since the jersey knit fabric has a tendency to curl up.

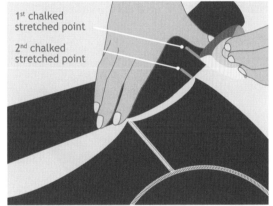

1st chalked stretched point

2nd chalked stretched point

step 5.4

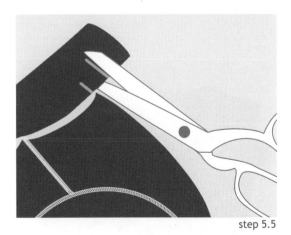

step 5.5

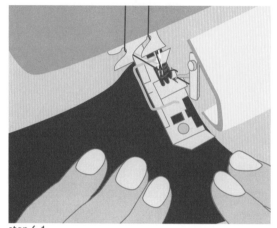
step 6.1

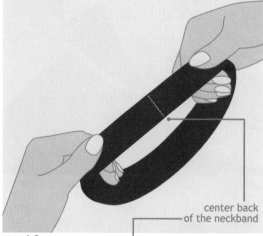
center back
of the neckband

step 6.2

step 6.4

6. Joining neckband to neck opening

6.1 Fold the band in half along its length, right sides facing in. Join the short ends of the neckband together with the overlocker. This is the center back of the neckband.

6.2 Fold the neckband in half along its width with the right sides facing out.

6.3 Match the seam on the neckband to the center back chalk mark, match the center front chalk mark on the neckband to the center front mark, and start pinning the band to the neckline with right sides matching.

6.4 Continue to pin the band into the neckline, matching the shoulder seams to the chalk marks on the neckband until it is completely pinned in place.

6.5 Sewing the neckband in correctly takes a little practice, so first sew the neckband in using a sewing machine. Remove the pins and then overlock it in place.

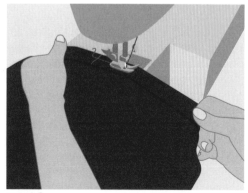
step 6.5

> **NOTE** Another nice finish for the neckline is a rolled-hem stitch. Instead of the separate neckband you can make this easy finish using the overlock machine.

7. Rolled hem on overlock machine
(alternative neckline finish)

7.1 Adjust your overlock machine to a rolled-hem finish. Remove the left needle and change the tension settings and stitch length. Refer to the manual that comes with the machine.

7.2 Start sewing at the shoulder seam and continue around the back of the T-shirt to the other shoulder seam and around the front, ending up at the starting shoulder seam.

7.3 As you reach the starting point, gradually sew over the beginning threads while easing the edge of the neckline out of the machine. Look down at the needles while you are doing this in order to create a clean-looking finish while easing the neckline out of the machine.

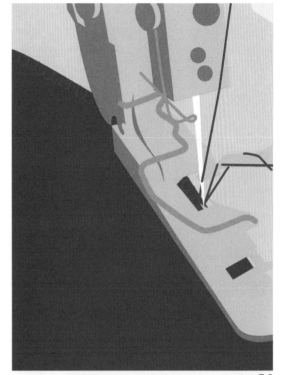

step 7.2

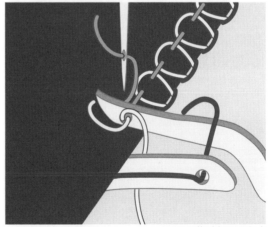

neat rolled-hem stitch

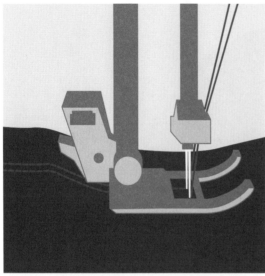

step 7.4

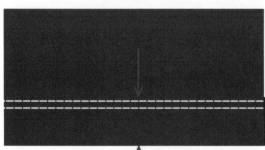

$^1/_2$ inch allowance
for sleeve hem

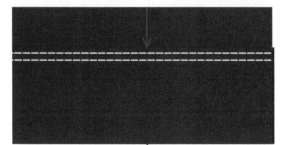

1 inch allowance
for bottom hem

7. Finishing the hem on sleeves and bottom edge

7.1 Before hemming, overlock the edge around the bottom of the T-shirt and sleeves.

7.2 Bend in a $^1/_2$ inch hem on sleeves and 1 inch hem on the bottom of the T-shirt and press with an iron.

> **EXPERT TIP**
> By using the sewing machine and stretch knit twin needles, you can achieve a professional looking finished hem on the sleeves and the bottom of the T-shirt.

7.3 Test the twin needles by sewing first on a leftover scrap of fabric.

7.4 Start sewing at the side seam of the hem and continue around the back to the front, ending at the side seam where you began.

> **NOTE** Make sure to sew the hem with the right sides of the T-shirt facing out in order that the twin needle effect shows to the best effect.

Your T-shirt is ready to wear.

CHECKLIST > > >

1. Fold selvages in toward the center of the fabric, check to make sure the measurement is consistent all the way down the length of the fabric on both sides and that the fabric is smoothly laid out.

2. Pin, cut, and chalk mark the notches at the center front and center back necklines and the front and back armholes.

3. Join shoulder seams.

4. Join sleeves to armholes.

5. Join side seams and underarm sleeves.

6. Check to make sure that the neckband is marked correctly to fit the neckline of your T-shirt.

7. Join the neckband to the neckline, making sure to stretch out the fabric and match the marks.

8. Sew the hems of the sleeves and the bottom on the right side of the T-shirt using twin needles and then press.

What you need to make it

Materials
2 yards of fabric for all sizes, 45 inches to 54 inches wide
1 small square of fusible tricot interfacing, $1\frac{1}{2}$ x $1\frac{1}{2}$ inches wide
All-purpose thread to match fabric
4 spools of overlock or serger thread to match fabric

Optional
4 yards of ribbon, $\frac{1}{2}$ inch wide

Fabric suggestions
Silk, silk chamois, polyester chamois. Only very drapey fabrics are good for this project.

Tools
Dotted pattern paper, brown Kraft paper, or unprinted newsprint paper — to put under fabric when cutting
Paper scissors
Fabric scissors
Dressmaker pins (size 17 or 20)
Clear ruler (2 x 18 inches long)
Tailor's chalk
Dressmaker's tracing wheel and tracing paper
Sewing machine and if available an overlock machine or serger
Iron and ironing board
Needle for hand sewing
Seam ripper

NOTE Make sure to measure your bust and check the size chart on page 127.

Skills you will learn
How to make a rolled-hem finish on the overlock machine
How to make string ties
How to sew tucks
How to make buttonholes

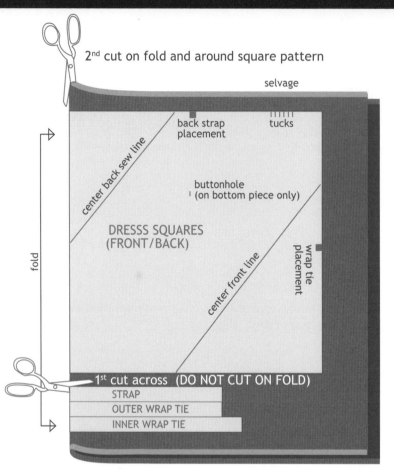

2ⁿᵈ cut on fold and around square pattern

selvage

back strap placement

tucks

center back sew line

buttonhole
ᴵ (on bottom piece only)

DRESSS SQUARES
(FRONT/BACK)

center front line

wrap tie placement

fold

1ˢᵗ cut across (DO NOT CUT ON FOLD)

STRAP

OUTER WRAP TIE

INNER WRAP TIE

1. Cutting instructions

Cut out the pattern pieces and pin the patterns to the fabric following the layout above.

> **NOTE** When using silk or any slippery fabric it's always best to put a layer of paper down and then lay the fabric on top of it. The paper keeps the fabric from slipping, making it easier to cut out the pattern accurately.

Cut: 2 squares for dress front and back
1 strap on fold
2 ties on fold
First cut across as shown in the layout. Cut out the strap and the two ties. Unfold these pieces. Then cut on the fold and around the pattern to make two squares for the front and back of the dress.

2. Checklist of notches to chalk mark

On each dress square:
1 back strap placement
1 wrap tie placement
On dress square right side only:
1 buttonhole

3. Before starting to sew

3.1 Mark all notches with tailor's chalk instead of clipping.

3.2 Chalk mark an "X" on all pattern pieces to indicate the wrong side of fabric.

3.3 Using a dressmaker's tracing wheel and tracing paper, mark the center back sew line and tuck lines, as indicated on pattern piece.

3.4 Unpin the pattern pieces.

4. Sewing the tucks

4.1 Following the traced lines for the three tucks, fold and pin them in place on each front side of the dress making sure they are folded in the same direction.

4.2 On the edge of each fold, topstitch each tuck down. Start sewing from the edge of the dress and continue, stopping at 1 inch.

5. Finishing the raw edges

5.1 All cut raw edges of the dress need to be finished after sewing the tucks. This keeps the fabric from stretching and fraying.

5.2 You can use either the rolled-hem setting on the overlock machine or a small zigzag stitch on the sewing machine to finish off all four sides of the squares.

Method A: overlock machine
(rolled-hem finish)

5.3 Adjust your overlock machine to a rolled-hem finish. Remove the left needle and change the tension settings and stitch length. Refer to the manual that comes with the machine.

5.4 A good setting for the rolled-hem on silk is a differential set at neutral (n). and the stitch length (should be close together) at 1 to 1.5.

> **NOTE** Test first on a piece of scrap fabric since it is important to get the correct stitch distance and settings. The right setting should keep the fabric from waving.

5.5 Finish off the raw edges of the two dress pieces.

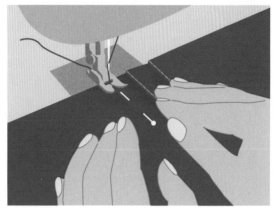

step 4.2

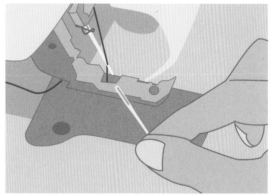

step 5.3

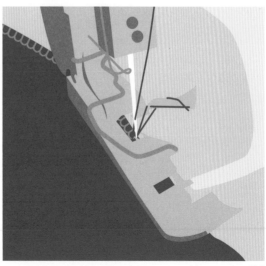

step 5.5

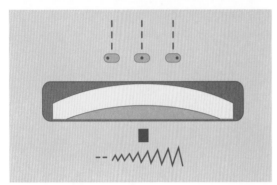

step 5.6

Method B: sewing machine
(zigzag stitch finish)

5.6 Adjust to a zigzag stitch.

5.7 A good setting for the zigzag stitch on silk is: stitch length 2 and stitch width 3.5.

> NOTE Always test the stitch first on a piece of scrap fabric and adjust the zigzag length and width if needed for coverage and a good looking finish. Each fabric performs differently.

5.8 Finish off the raw edges of the two dress pieces.

6. Joining the dress

6.1 With right sides facing pin the traced center back lines together. Sew along this seam by machine. Cut away the excess fabric, making sure to leave at least ½ inch seam allowance from the sewing line.

6.2 Overlock the seam with either rolled-hem stitch or small zigzag stitch (as previously).

7. Make one buttonhole for inner tie

> NOTE Make a test buttonhole on a scrap piece of fabric first.

7.1 On the right side mark ½ inch length buttonhole on the dress. Follow the buttonhole mark on the dress pattern.

7.2 On wrong side, iron a 1½ inch square of fusible onto the marked buttonhole placement. This will keep the button-hole from stretching.

7.2 Make buttonhole following your sewing machine instruction manual.

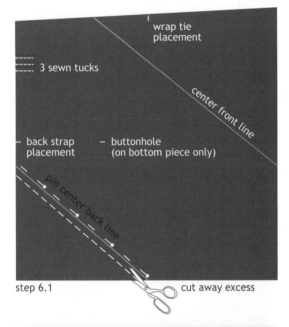

wrap tie placement

3 sewn tucks

center front line

back strap placement

buttonhole (on bottom piece only)

pin center back line

step 6.1

cut away excess

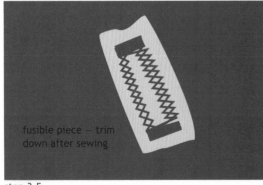

fusible piece – trim down after sewing

step 3.5

7.3 Carefully cut open the buttonhole with a seam ripper. Before cutting open the buttonhole, place a pin at the end of the hole so you won't cut past the threads while opening it.

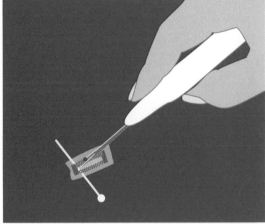

step 7.3

8. Sewing the straps and the wrap ties

8.1 With right side up lay the ribbon over the strap parallel to lengthwise edge. Pin one end of ribbon to the short end of the strap to hold in place.

8.2 Fold the right sides of the strap together over the ribbon with the raw edges meeting to enclose the ribbon. Sew the strap together along the lengthwise edge close to the raw edges and along one short end over the ribbon using $1/2$ inch seam allowance.

8.3 Be careful not to sew over the ribbon inside the strap.

8.4 To turn strap to right side, pull on end of ribbon while holding strap at the other end where the ribbon is attached.

8.5 Gradually keep pulling and strap will turn to the right side. Cut away the ribbon and with an iron press the strap.

8.6 Fold the strap in half and cut it at the fold to make two shoulder straps.

8.7 Repeat steps 8.1 to 8.5 to make the two wrap ties. DO NOT cut in half.

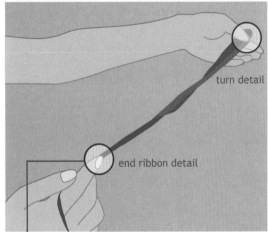

turn detail

end ribbon detail

step 8.4

NOTE If you don't want to sew the fabric straps and ties, substitute $1/2$ inch wide ribbon instead.

turn detail

end ribbon detail

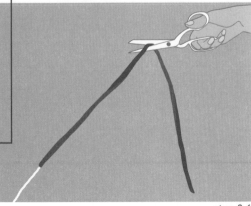

step 8.6

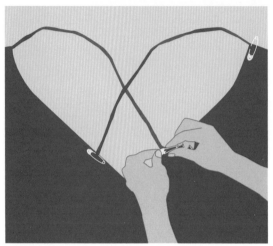

step 9.1

9. Finishing the dress

9.1 Pin or safety pin the straps to the top points of the halter front and to the chalk marks on inside the back of the dress. Pin wrap ties to chalk marks on the front of the dress.

9.2 Before sewing the straps in place, try on the dress to check and see if the straps need to be adjusted to fit your shoulders.

9.3 By hand, with a needle and thread, attach the end of the straps to the top points of the halter front and then to the back placement on the dress.

Your dress is ready to wear and you are ready to go out and party.

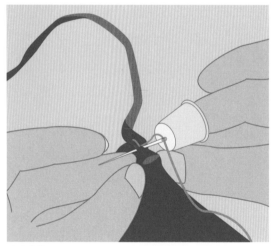

step 9.3

CHECK LIST >>>

1. This dress looks best in silk or a slippery fabric.

2. Be sure to use paper under slippery fabrics for ease in cutting.

3. Check that all chalk mark are made for tucks, straps, ties, and buttonhole placement.

4. Test the rolled-hem or zigzag stitch finish on a scrap of fabric before sewing.

5. When sewing skinny straps use a ribbon sewn inside the strap to pull and turn straps to the right side.

6. Use fusible tricot interfacing for reinforcement and to make a nicely finished buttonhole.

7. Try on the dress to make sure the straps are the right length across your shoulders before stitching them in place.

What you need to make it

Materials
One small lambskin, about 2 x 2 1/2 feet wide
Heavyweight fusible interfacing, 1/2 yard
Polyester satin lining fabric, 1/2 yard (can be solid or a print)
100% polyester upholstery thread
Magnetic snap used for accessories

> **NOTE** Lambskin is supple and one of the easiest leathers to sew.
> Before cutting inspect the skin for holes and thin spots, which are
> usually found in neck and leg areas. Do not include those areas in
> your holder as they are fragile and can easily tear. Lambskin, like all
> leathers, has flaws and is unevenly shaped. As it is sold by the square
> foot there might be some leftover scraps.

Other fabric suggestions
1/2 yard faux leather or suede, 45 inches wide

Tools
Paper scissors
Rotary cutter and cutting mat
Clear ruler or metal ruler
Tailor's chalk and pencil
Double-stick tape
Glue stick
Dry iron (do not put water in it)
Sewing machine
Teflon all-purpose foot

Skills you will learn
How to cut and sew leather or faux leather
How to put in magnetic snaps
How to fuse interfacing

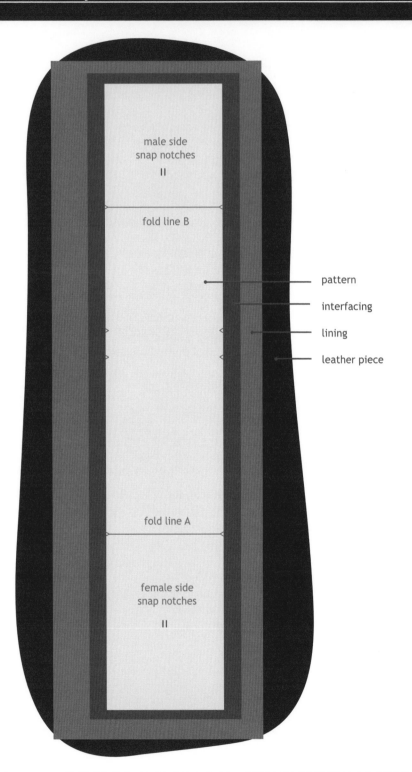

male side
snap notches

||

fold line B

pattern

interfacing

lining

leather piece

fold line A

female side
snap notches

||

1. Cutting instructions

1.1 Cut out the pattern piece.

1.2 For leather or fake leather, hold the paper pattern in place by using double-stick tape as follows: on the wrong side of the pattern place little strips of double-stick tape in all four corners and in the center. Press pattern on the right side of the lambskin.

1.3 Use a rotary cutter, mat, and ruler to cut out the holder. To ensure a clean straight line, place the ruler at the edge of the pattern where you are cutting to guide the rotary cutter. Always cut away from yourself to avoid an accident.

1.4 Pin the pattern to both the lining and heavyweight fusible interfacing and cut both out at the same time using the rotary cutter or scissors.

2. Fusing interfacing to leather

> NOTE Before making the actual project it's best to test fuse the interfacing to the leather in order to see how hot the iron can be and how much heat the leather or fake leather can take. DO NOT ADD WATER TO THE IRON. Use a dry iron on the cotton setting.

2.1 Using a dry iron on the cotton setting (don't forget to let the iron warm up) lay the interfacing glue-side down on the wrong side of the leather and fuse using the iron. Adjust temperature if necessary. Let cool after fusing.

2.2 Test the fusible and leather to see if they are firmly stuck together.

2.3 Trim any excess interfacing extending outside the edge of the leather piece.

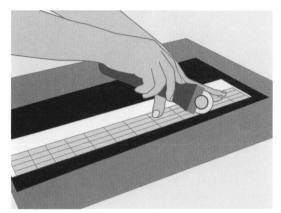

step 1.3

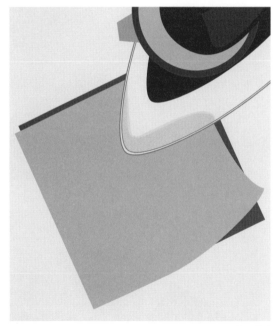

step 2.1

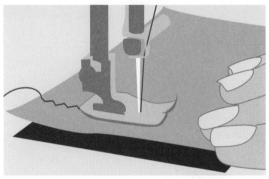

step 3.3

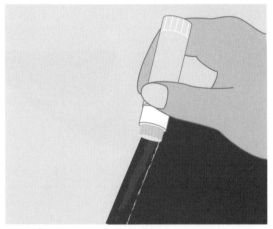

step 4.2

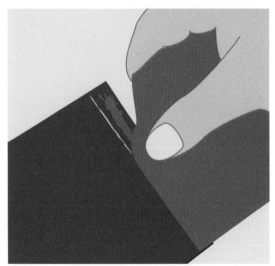

step 4.3

3. Before starting to sew

3.1 Change to a Teflon foot on your sewing machine and thread the machine with 100% polyester thread.

3.2 Set the machine to make a zigzag stitch, length 3 and width 3, and increase the tension to 9.

3.3 Always test your stitching on a scrap piece of leather and interfacing that you have previously fused. Do several tests, working on both a single layer and double layer of leather.

3.4 Do not pull piece through the machine. If it is getting stuck, adjust your stitch length to a larger size.

4. Gluing upper edge of lining to holder

4.1 With the interfacing side faceup, rule a ½ inch seam allowance at the top end of the holder by marking a chalk line directly on the interfacing.

4.2 Run the glue stick over the end of the holder inside the seam allowance line just marked.

4.3 Place the right side of the lining over the glued edge, lining it up on the chalked line. Finger press the lining in place.

5. Sewing lining to holder

5.1 Flatten out both pieces.

5.2 With the right side of the leather faceup, sew the holder and the lining together using a zigzag stitch—stitching down where the fabric joins. Sew over the edges of both the leather and the lining.

> EXPERT TIP When sewing leather, DO NOT use the reverse stitch.

5.3 Leave 7 inches of extra thread so you can tie and knot the threads at the end of each seam. After knotting, trim the ends to no longer than ¼ inch.

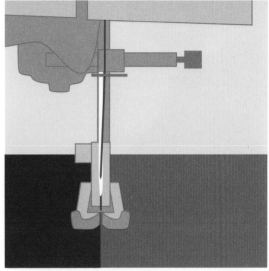

step 5.2

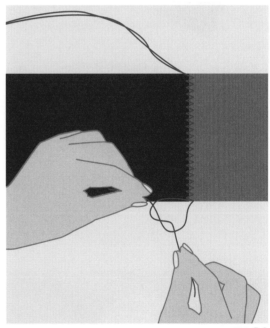

step 5.3

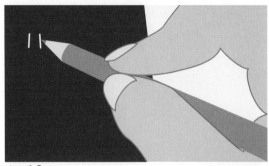

step 6.2

step 6.3

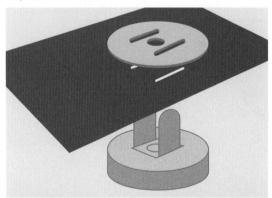

step 6.5 — start

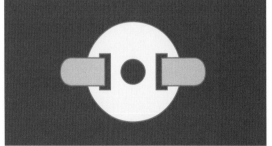

step 6.5 — finish

6. Inserting the magnetic snap

6.1 Place your paper pattern on the front side of the holder, taking care to match the top with the stitched edge.

6.2 Make pencil marks on the holder, following the marks on the pattern, for the female and male closures.

6.3 Using the tips of your scissors, stab through the holder and clip small slashes where the holder is marked.

6.4 Insert the male closure into the flap side of the holder, and the female closure into other side with prongs facing up on the interfacing side.

6.5 On the interfacing side of the holder, slide the washers over the prongs and press the prongs away from each other with your fingers.
(Refer also to the instructions with the closures).

7. Gluing the rest of the lining to the holder

7.1 Run the glue stick around all the edges of interfaced side of the holder, then go over the remaining area with the glue.

7.2 Flip the lining over the sewn edge, pull and press it evenly down over the glued area, working your way down from the sewn edge to the open edge.

> **NOTE** The lining has a tendency to distort a bit, often extending over the sides. Trim any excess lining away from the sides of the holder. The lining deliberately does not reach the open edge end. Don't worry since this part won't show.

7.3 Place the paper pattern over the lining side of the holder and chalk or pencil mark the notches for fold line A. Take care to match the top of the pattern to the sewn edge of the holder.

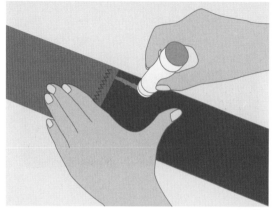

step 7.1

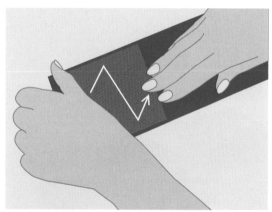

step 7.2

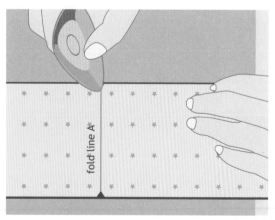

step 7.3

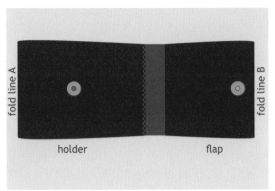

steps 8.1–8.2

8. Making the holder and the flap

8.1 Fold on line A, matching the lining sides face-in to make the body of the holder.

8.2 Fold on line B, matching the lining sides face-in to make the flap of the holder.

9. Joining the holder and the flap

9.1 Join the sides together by zigzag stitching along each long side of both holder and flap.

> **IMPORTANT** Be sure to continue to sew to the end of the holder to close up the sides completely for a finished look. Knot the ends of the thread at all edges.

Your iPod holder is ready to use.

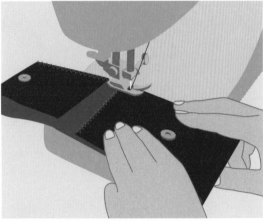

step 9.1

CHECKLIST >>>

1. Check the lambskin for holes or irregular areas before cutting.

2. Use a rotary cutter and a mat to cut the leather or faux leather.

3. When fusing the facing, make sure to use a dry iron.

4. Trim off any of the lining edges that extend over the sides of the holder.

5. Use a Teflon all-purpose foot and test sew a fused piece of leather or faux leather before sewing.

6. Use a glue stick to glue the lining in place.

7. Be sure to carefully fold the holder according to the pattern.

8. Sew the edges of the holder and the flap, then knot the ends at all corners.

This project starts as a single box cushion, and by joining three of them it can be used folded up as an ottoman or open as a small sleeping mattress. The cover is a nice finishing touch. Read the instructions before you begin, so you completely understand how these three cushions are assembled and joined together to make the ottoman.

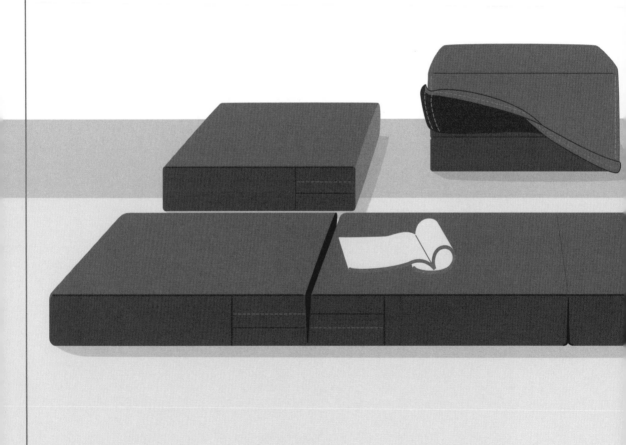

What you need to make it

Materials

For one box cushion
2 yards of fabric, 48 to 54 inches wide
1 zipper (preferably 4.5 size upholstery zipper with a closed bottom), 31 inches long
1 high-density foam block, 22 x 22 inches square and 4 inches deep

For three box cushions (ottoman) and cover
6 yards of fabric, 48 to 54 inches wide.
3 zippers (preferably 4.5 size upholstery zippers with closed bottoms), 31 inches long
3 high density foam blocks, 22 x 22 inches square and 4 inches deep

Fabric suggestions

Heavyweight cottons, denim, or other upholstery fabrics, as long as they are not too thick to sew easily. Don't use plaids or directional prints, stretch fabrics, loosely woven fabrics that unravel, velvet, or fake fur.

Tools

Paper scissors
Fabric scissors
Dressmaker pins (size 17 or 20)
Clear ruler (2 x 18 inches long)
Tape measure
Tailor's chalk
Sewing machine
Sewing machine needles (size 12 or 14)
Magnetic seam guide
Iron and ironing board

Skills you will learn

How to sew a lapped zipper
How to work with heavier fabric
How to sew and turn corners accurately

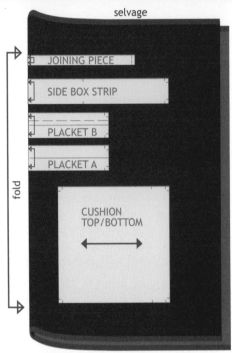

Layout A — pattern layout box cushion

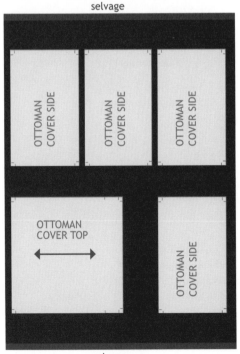

Layout B
— pattern layout
for ottoman cover

1. Cutting instructions

1.1 For making one box cushion only
— follow Layout A

Cut: 1 cushion top
1 cushion bottom
1 side box strip
1 placket A
1 placket B

1.2 For three joined box cushions (ottoman)
— follow Layout A

Cut: 3 cushion top
3 cushion bottom
3 side box strip
3 placket A
3 placket B
2 joining piece

1.3 For ottoman cover
— follow Layout B

Cut: 1 ottoman cover top
4 ottoman cover side

2. Checklist of notches to clip

10 notches on each cushion top
10 notches on each cushion bottom
12 notches on each side box strip
8 notches on each placket A
8 notches on each placket B
8 notches on ottoman cover top
8 notches on ottoman cover sides

Clip all your notches using the tips
of your scissors.

3. Before unpinning the paper patterns

3.1 Follow the printed text on the patterns to carefully chalk mark your cut pieces on the wrong side of the fabric.

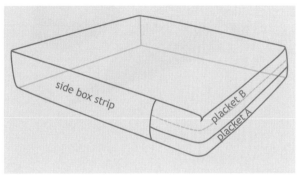

3.2 For one box cushion only
— see fig. 1
Chalk mark:
cushion top
cushion bottom
placket A
placket B
side box strip

fig. 1 — one box cushion

3.3 For three joined box cushions (ottoman) — see fig. 2

Mark: top cushion:
  cushion top [1A]
  cushion bottom [1B]
  placket [1A]
  placket [1B]
  side box strip [1]
Mark: middle cushion:
  cushion top [2A]
  cushion bottom [2B]
  placket [2A]
  placket [2B]
  side box strip [2]
Mark: bottom cushion:
  cushion top [3A]
  cushion bottom [3B]
  placket [3A]
  placket [3B]
  side box strip [3]

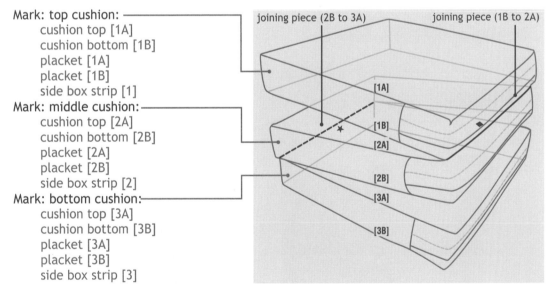

fig. 2 — three joined box cushions (ottoman)

Mark: **one star symbol** where indicated on cushion bottom [2B] and where indicated on each joining piece.
Mark: **one diamond symbol** where indicated on cushion top [2A] and where indicated on each joining pieces.
Mark: words "zipper side" on [1B] and [3A]
Mark: an "X" on all pattern pieces to indicate the wrong side of fabric.

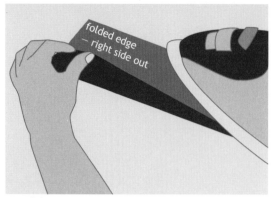

step 4.1

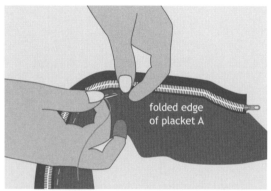

step 5.1

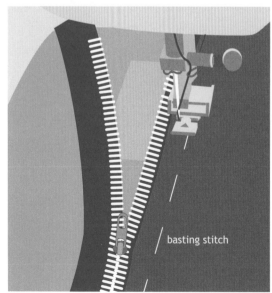

step 5.3

4. Preparing the lapped zipper

4.1 Unpin placket B and fold in half length-wise, with the right sides facing out, then press.

4.2 Rule a chalk line as indicated on the pattern placket B, 1 inch from the fold line.

4.3 Unpin placket A and fold in half length-wise, with the right sides facing out, then press.

5. Sewing the lapped zipper

5.1 Pin the zipper to the folded edge of placket A, making sure that the teeth of the zipper are placed close along the folded edge and the zipper pull is facing you. Using a basting stitch, hand sew this side of the zipper in place on right side of placket. Remove pins before machine sewing.

5.2 On the sewing machine change the all-purpose foot to a zipper foot making sure the position of the zipper foot side allows you to sew as close to the zipper teeth as possible.

5.3 Machine stitch very close along side of the zipper teeth. Sew the zipper in place beginning at the top end and continue to sew to the end with the clamp on the zipper. Stop sewing just after reaching the metal clamp.

NOTE Make sure to sew a reverse stitch when starting and finishing all seams to lock the stitching.

5.4 Pin the unsewn side of the zipper to placket B, placing the placket so that it covers the zipper and the chalk line falls along the teeth in order to conceal the zipper and create the lap. Using a basting stitch, hand sew the zipper in place. Remove pins before machine sewing.

5.5 On the sewing machine, change the zipper foot position from the side it's on to the other side in order to sew close along side of the zipper teeth again.

5.6 After zipper is sewn in place remove the basting stitch.

> **NOTE** When you're sewing the zipper in place you will need to stop and pull the zipper pull down to get it out of the way of the needle. Sew the zipper halfway and then put the needle down into the fabric, pick up the pressure foot and pull the zipper pull up and out of the way. Continue sewing.

6. Sewing the cushion side

6.1 Change back to an all-purpose foot.

6.2 With right sides facing, pin and sew the side box strip to both ends of the zipper placket. You now have one continuous piece that forms the cushion side.

> **EXPERT TIP** If you have to sew across the zipper teeth, sew very slowly so you don't break the needle.

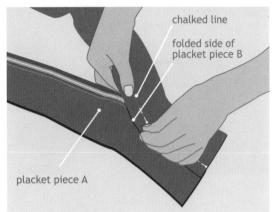

chalked line

folded side of placket piece B

placket piece A

step 5.4

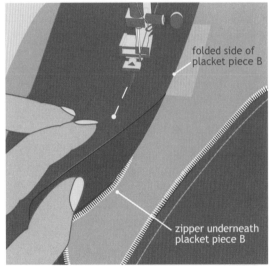

folded side of placket piece B

zipper underneath placket piece B

step 5.5

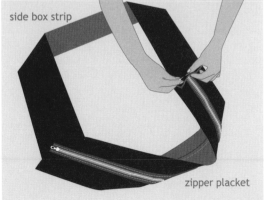

side box strip

zipper placket

step 6.2 — cushion side

step 7.3

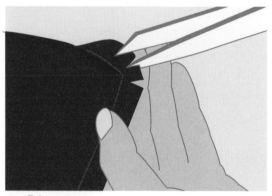

step 7.6

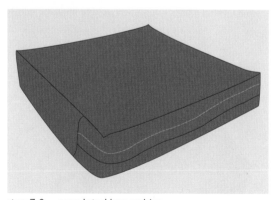

step 7.8 — completed box cushion

7. Sewing the cushion side to the cushion top and bottom

7.1 Pin the cushion side to the cushion top with right sides facing, making sure to match the notches. Your zipper should be closed at this point.

7.2 Start sewing at the point where the zipper placket is sewn to the side box strip and continue up to the corner of the cushion top.

7.3 Lower the needle of machine down into the corner, pick up the presser foot, and turn the corner 90 degrees around to the next side. Clip the cushion side at the corner to make it lay flat.

7.4 Put your presser foot down and continue sewing around until you end up where you started, turning all corners as above.

7.5 Repeat steps 7.1–7.4 to attach cushion side to the cushion bottom but make sure this time to unzip the zipper before sewing.

7.6 You will need to snip into the corners of the top and bottom pieces with your scissors so they will lie flat.

7.7 Turn your cushion right side out. Use the tips of the scissors to push the corners out from the wrong side and then press the cushion cover.

7.8 Insert a foam block into the cushion and close zipper.

Your box cushion is now completed. Follow steps 8–12 if you want to make the ottoman, or mattress.

8. Making three cushion sides

8.1 Repeat steps 4–6 so that you have three completed cushion sides.

9. Making the two joining pieces to attach the cushions together

9.1 Sew the short ends together of one joining piece, right sides in. This will form a circle. Turn right side out.

9.2 Press flat so this seam falls in the center of the strip. There will be raw edges on both long sides.

9.3 Repeat steps 9.1–9.2 for the second joining piece.

10. Assembling the middle cushion

10.1 With right sides facing, pin one joining piece to the cushion top [2A] matching diamond symbols on joining piece and cushion top.

> NOTE After sewing in place, the joining pieces will stick out on the right side of the middle cushion.
> (See step 10.10 on page 106 to see completed step).

10.2 As you sew the joining piece to the cushion top [2A], remove the pins.

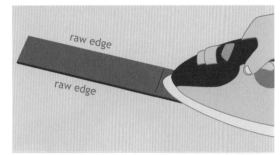

step 9.2

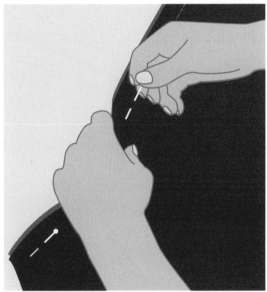

step 10.1

step 10.2

step 10.4

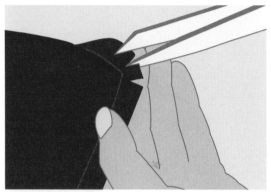

step 10.8

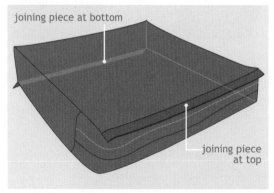

joining piece at bottom

joining piece at top

step 10.10 — middle cushion with joining strips

10.3 Pin the cushion side to the cushion top [2A] with the right sides facing, making sure to match the notches and joining piece sandwiched in between. Your zipper should be closed at this point.

10.4 Repeat steps 7.2—7.4 to sew the cushion side to cushion top [2A].

10.5 With right sides facing, pin the second joining piece to the cushion bottom [2B] matching star symbols on joining piece and cushion bottom. Sew in place.

10.6 Pin the cushion side to the cushion bottom [2B] with the right sides facing, making sure to match the notches and joining piece sandwiched in between. Make sure this time to unzip the zipper before sewing.

10.7 Repeat steps 7.2—7.4 to sew the cushion side to cushion bottom [2B].

10.8 You will need to snip into corners of the top and bottom pieces with your scissors so they will lie flat.

10.9 Turn your cushion right side out. Use the tips of the scissors to push the corners out from the wrong sides and then press the cushion cover.

10.10 When completed, your middle cushion will have a joining strip sticking out of the top of the cushion and out of the bottom opposite side.

11. Assembling the top cushion

11.1 With the right sides facing, pin the raw edge of the joining piece attached to cushion top [2A] to the side with the zipper on cushion bottom [1B]. Sew in place.

11.2 Pin the cushion side with placket A to the cushion bottom [1B], with right sides facing and joining piece sandwiched in between. Match the notches and pin with right sides facing. Keep the zipper closed.

11.3 Sew in place following steps 7.2—7.4.

11.4 Pin the cushion side to the cushion top [1A], with right sides facing and following steps 7.2—7.4 to complete cushion. Make sure to keep the zipper open.

11.5 You will need to snip into corners of the top and bottom pieces with your scissors so they will lie flat.

11.6 Turn your cushion right side out. Use the tips of the scissors to push the corners out from the wrong side and then press the cushion cover.

11.7 You now have the top cushion and the middle cushion joined to each other and completely sewn together.

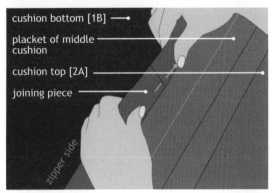

cushion bottom [1B]
placket of middle cushion
cushion top [2A]
joining piece
zipper side

step 11.1

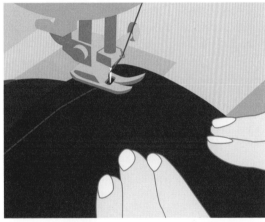

step 11.3

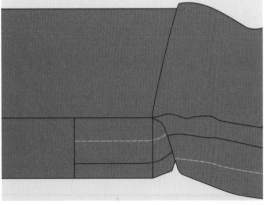

step 11.7

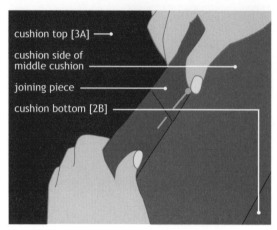

cushion top [3A] ⎯

cushion side of
middle cushion ⎯

joining piece ⎯

cushion bottom [2B] ⎯

step 12.1

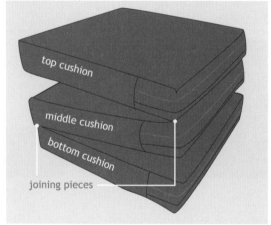

top cushion

middle cushion

bottom cushion

joining pieces ⎯

step 12.5 — three joined cushions to make an ottoman

12. Assembling the bottom cushion

12.1 With the right sides facing, pin the raw edge of the joining piece attached to cushion bottom [2B] to the cushion top [3A] on the side opposite the zipper. Sew in place.

12.2 Pin the cushion side with placket B to cushion top [3A], right sides facing and joining piece sandwiched in between. Keep the zipper closed. Sew in place following steps 7.2–7.4.

12.3 Pin the cushion side to the cushion bottom [3B], with right sides facing and following steps 7.2–7.4 to complete bottom cushion. Make sure to keep the zipper open.

12.4 Snip into corners of the top and bottom pieces with your scissors so they will lie flat.

12.5 Turn your cushion right side out. Use the tips of the scissors to push the corners out from the wrong side and then press the cushion cover.

12.6 You now have all three box cushions joined to each other.

12.7 Insert the foam blocks into all three cushions and close zippers.

Stacked above each other the box cushions become an ottoman or, when opened out, a small sleeping mattress.

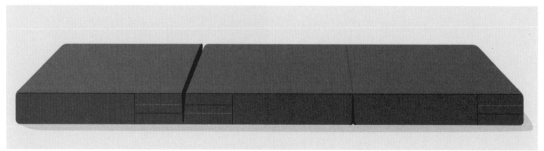

three joined cushions opened out to make a sleeping mattress

13. Assembling the ottoman cover

13.1 With right sides facing, pin and sew the two ottoman cover side pieces to each other, on the short side, using a ½ inch seam allowance. Repeat for remaining sides so they are joined together.

13.2 Press all the seam allowances open.

13.3 Sew along both sides of each four seam edges, ¼ inch from the seam, using the side of the all-purpose foot as a guide.

> **EXPERT TIP** This top stitch on either side of the seam holds back and strengthens the seam allowance as well as adds a design detail to the cover.

13.4 With right sides facing, pin the top cover to the side pieces, matching the corner notches on all four sides.

13.5 Start sewing at one corner and continue to sew to the next corner of the square.

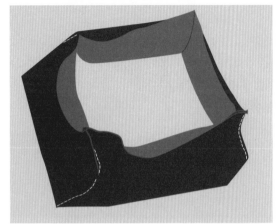

step 13.1 – all four cover sides joined together

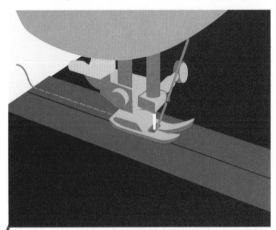

step 13.3 – sewn on wrong side

step 13.3 detail
on right side

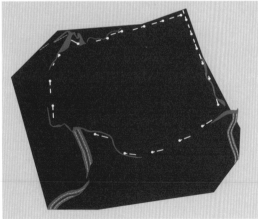

step 13.4

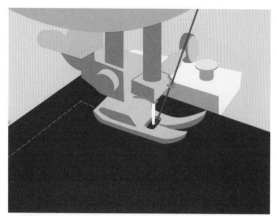

step 13.6

13.6 Lower the needle of the machine down into the corner, pick up the presser foot, and turn the corner of the pillow square around 90 degrees to the next side of the pillow. Then put your presser foot down and continue sewing to where you began.

13.7 Turn the cover right side out. Use the tips of the scissors to push the corners out from the wrong side.

13.8 You will need to snip into corners of the top piece with your scissors so it will lie flat.

13.9 Press the ottoman cover.

13.10 At the bottom, press a double folded hem so no raw edges are showing. Sew the hem on the wrong side.

13.11 Put the cover on the folded cushions.

Your ottoman with cover is a new piece of furniture for your home. It can be used as a foot stool or, with a tray on top, a coffee table.

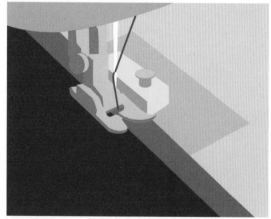

step 13.9

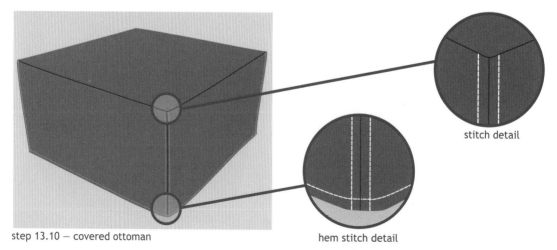

step 13.10 — covered ottoman

stitch detail

hem stitch detail

CHECKLIST > > >

(1) Decide if you want to make a box cushion or the more complicated ottoman with cover.

(2) Read the instructions before you begin, so you completely understand how three cushions are assembled and joined together to make the ottoman.

(3) Make sure that you cut all the pattern pieces out before you begin to sew.

(4) Check to see if you clipped all the notches.

(5) Follow the printed text on the patterns to carefully chalk mark your cut pieces on the wrong side of the fabric.

(6) Baste the lapped zipper in place before sewing.

(7) Make sure the two joining pieces are pinned to the correct places on the middle cushion pieces before sewing. See positioning on fig. 2 on page 101 if you are confused.

(8) After turning your cushions right side out, use the tips of the scissors to push the corners out from the wrong side.

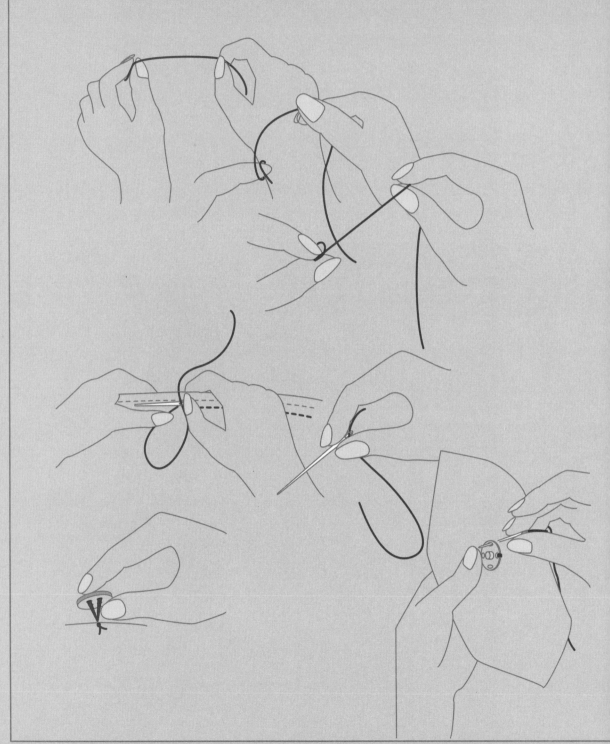

Needles

When sewing by hand you need to have good needles appropriate for the job you're doing. For instance, if you are sewing a very heavy fabric then you need a tapestry needle to help you get through the fabric. Your assorted pack of needles will have many different sizes for you to choose from.

A thimble is also very helpful in pushing the needle through the fabric. It takes a while to get accustomed to using a thimble but it makes sewing faster and improves your hand sewing skills.

Making a knot

To make a knot at the end of your thread before you start to sew:

1 Hold the end of the thread in your hands.
2 Twist the end of the thread twice around the first finger of your hand, and with your thumb roll it off the finger.
3 Pull the thread down between thumb and finger, and at the end will be a small knot.

Knotted threads are used to prevent stitches from pulling out as you work. You can also make two small stitches, one over the other, to keep the threads from slipping out at both the beginning and end of basting stitches.

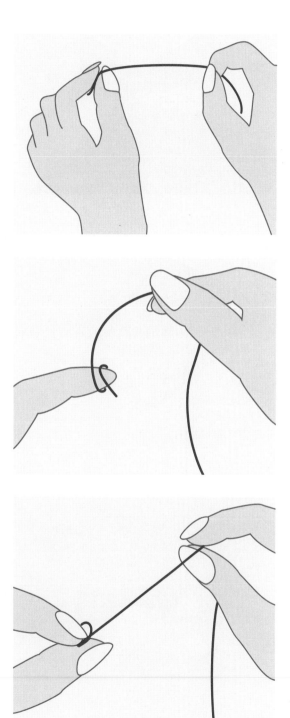

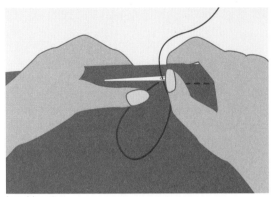

hand basting

Hand basting

Hand basting is a series of temporary stitches made in a straight line, used to hold two or more layers of fabric in place or together.

A basting stitch is very helpful when sewing in zippers. Sometimes this old phrase applies, "A stitch in time saves nine." Basting stitches are even stitches about $1/2$ to $5/8$ inch long, that are sewn by going in one side of the fabric and out the other side and then back into the side you started the stitching on. Make sure to keep the stitches even—one after the other in line. When ready to sew, machine stitch in the same place over the basting.

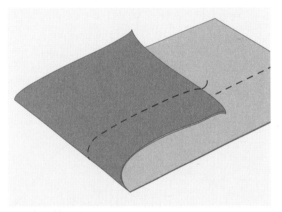

even hand basting

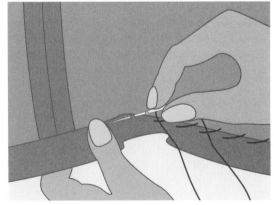

hand hemming

Hand hemming

Hand hemming using a blind hemstitch is a sign of a more expensive garment. It is not noticeable on the right side. Also, this hem makes a garment hang better than a machine sewn hem.

You do this by taking a tiny stitch into the garment and a tiny stitch onto the edge of the hem. Train yourself to catch only a few threads on the fabric of the right side of the garment. Most hems are made with stitches that are about $1/2$ inch in length and slanted.

Sewing on a button

In order to sew on a button so that it won't come off, use a thicker thread. This kind of thread is called button or carpet thread. This thread has a tendency to knot while you are sewing. In order to avoid this happening, you can run the thread through some beeswax.

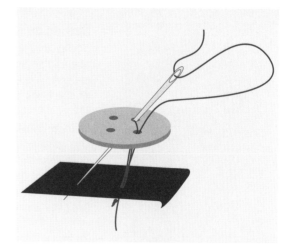

Buttons come with two or four holes in the center. You need to sew it on by making a shank to ease wear and tear so the button won't fall off. The length of the shank depends on the thickness of the fabric that the button is sewn onto.

1. Mark placement of button with a pencil mark. Make sure your thread knot is on the wrong side of your fabric. Pull the thread all the way through the fabric until the knot stops it.

2. Slide the button through the hole and onto the needle and thread, being careful to keep the right side of the button facing you. Push the needle through an adjacent hole and pull the thread tight, until you are holding the button ½ inch above the fabric. Push the needle through to the wrong side of the fabric while maintaining your ½ inch shank. Repeat this two or three times before continuing to the next pair of holes. Do the same on this pair.

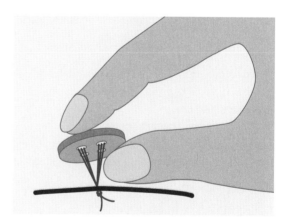

3. On the last stitch, as you go back down through the hole of the button toward the wrong side of the fabric, take your remaining thread and wrap it a number of times around those threads under the button to form the shank. When the shank feels stiff and secure, knot your thread on the wrong side of the fabric.

Using this technique, you will never lose a button.

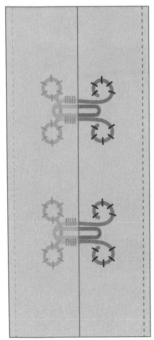

eye   hook

hooks and eyes open

hooks and eyes closed
(partially hidden)

Sewing on hooks and eyes

Hooks and eyes are made in matched pairs and generally used to secure waistbands and necklines. When the hook is caught in the eye, the edges of the garment meet and none of the hook fastening shows.

With a knotted thread sew the hook to the inside edge of the garment to hold it firmly in place. Sew through each hole several times then slide the needle through the fabric to the end of the hook and overcast a few stitches to secure the head of the hook to the garment and knot off to finish. Sew the eye onto the opposite edge right side of garment.

To mark the eye placement, overlap the garment and mark the position using the head of the hook as a guide. Use a pencil mark.

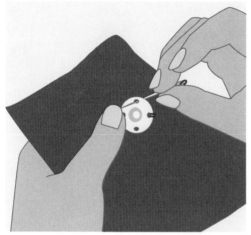

female snap (socket)

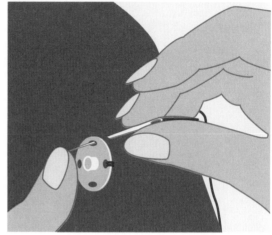

male snap (ball)

Sewing on snaps

Snaps are made in matched pairs and are used as a relaxed closure that has no strain. Snaps are generally hidden closures but in today's fashion can be exposed . The male side is called the ball side, it has an extending bump and the female side, called the socket, has a concave section.

Pencil mark the placement of the ball side and place the snap on the center of the placement. With a knotted thread, sew through each hole of the snap three times and end off the thread on the underside of the snap. To mark the placement of the socket side, rub a little chalk on the ball tip and then press down where the socket side should be. Sew the socket side down covering the marked placement. Sew through each hole three times ending with the thread on the underside of the snap. Knot off to finish.

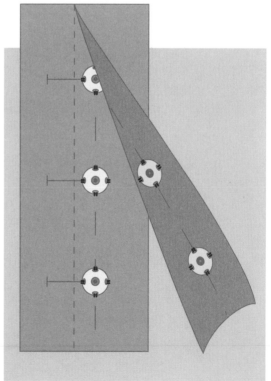

matching your snaps

A-line Appliqué Backstitch Basting Beeswax Bias Blindhem Bobbin Bobbin Calendering Casing Center back Center back symbol Clean finish Clip Cording Cross grain Cutting lines Darning Darts Drape Ease Fabric Facing Piece Fastener Feed dogs Fiber Fold False tape Flounce Fray Fusible Grain Hem Hemline Interfacing Join Knits Length Lockstitch Mitered corners Needle Notch Notions Overlocker Placket Parallel Pins Polyester Rolled hem Ruching Seam Selvage Serger Shirr Snap fastenings Stitch length Straight grain Tailor's ham Tapestry Tracing Tencel Thread Viscose wheel Velcro Warp Weft Yardstick Yarn Yoke Zipper foot

A-line A silhouette shape of a simple skirt, fitted at the hip and flaring wider at the hemline.

Adjustment line A double line printed on a pattern to indicate where to take in or out and lengthen or shorten.

All-purpose foot The basic foot on all sewing machines generally used for all sewing projects. Can be changed to other feet used for special purposes, such as sewing in a zipper.

Alter
To change the fit of a garment or pattern.

Appliqué A decoration that is sewn, glued, or fused onto another fabric.

Baby hem A small hem, approximately $1/4$ inch wide, often used as a hem finish on skirts, tablecloths, and napkins. It can be made by attaching a baby hem foot to the sewing machine.

Backstitch or **Back-tack** A reverse stitch on the sewing machine or by hand to keep the sewn seam from opening.

Basting A temporary stitch that can be made either by hand or machine sewn to hold fabrics in place temporarily. Machine basting is used to sew up a garment for a fitting.

Beeswax A hard wax used to keep hand sewing thread from knotting. Pull the thread along the beeswax to coat the thread.

Bias A diagonal line across the fabric. True bias is a 45% angle running from warp or weft that forms a diagonal across the fabric. It is the softest and most drapey way to cut fabric.

Bias tape Made from the bias cut of the fabric. It will sew around corners easily and is used to finish off a raw edge or a seam. You can buy packets ready-cut in different colors and widths.

Blind hem A hand stitch that doesn't show on the right side of the garment and keeps the hem in place. Blind hems can be made on a sewing machine if there is a stitch setting for it. It helps to have a blind hem foot.

Bobbin A small round spool that thread is wound onto, made out of plastic or metal. The bobbin goes into a case that is either part of the machine or separate and then put into the machine. Bobbins come in different classes. A class 15 bobbin is used for many machines. Always check to see that you are using the right size for your specific machine.

Bobbin case This holds the bobbin in the sewing machine; it is located in a compartment underneath the needle plate.

Bolt A unit in which fabric is packaged by the manufacturer and sold to fabric stores.

Calendering A finishing technique that polishes fabric to a smooth, shiny, lustrous finish. Cotton fabrics sometimes have this finish.

Casing A tunnel of fabric made by folding over the edge of the fabric through which a drawstring cord, elastic, or ribbon is

threaded. Usually used on pants, skirts or backpacks. A curtain rod can be inserted into the casing of a curtain as well.

Catch stitch A hand stitch made in a cross-stitch formation. It is especially used for hems on the bottoms of bridal wear and costumes. Its purpose is to prevent your heel from being caught in the hem.

Center back The place on a pattern (usually indicated with an arrow) or garment indicating the exact vertical center back.

Center front The place on a pattern (usually indicated with an arrow) or garment indicating the exact vertical center front.

Clean finish Any method (zigzag stitch, overlocked, or turned under) used to finish the raw edges of seams, hems or facings.

Clip A small cut with the tips of scissors into the seam allowance of fabric. Used to mark notches or help release strain on curved seams such as necklines, also used at corners to allow sharp points.

Cord stop A small plastic device that locks a drawstring in place.

Cross grain Also called the weft, these are the threads that run horizontally across the fabric from selvage to selvage. The term can also be used for knits.

Cutting lines The lines on a pattern that denote sizes. When choosing your cutting line, remember larger is better and pattern sizes do not reflect your clothing size. You should first take your measurements before choosing which size.

Decorative stitches Many sewing machines have decorative stitches that can create a special design effect. Experiment with them to see if you like the design they make on a project you're sewing.

Darning To repair small holes, rips, and worn areas in fabric by hand sewing or machine sewing.

Darts A triangle that tapers to a point and fits the garment to the curve of the body. Usually used at the side seam of blouses or on skirts, pants, and dresses to create shape.

Drape How fabric hangs. The thickness, sheer quality, fiber content, and how the fabric is cut will determine the way the fabric hangs.

Ease The slightly extra allowance or fullness given to a pattern or garment to allow for movement and sitting.

Ease stitch The even distribution of slightly extra fullness planned in a pattern when of section of a seam is joined to a slightly shorter seam but doesn't form gathers or tucks. It's just eased into place using the feed dogs of the machine and your fingers to hold it in place.

Edge stitch A sewn line that is $1/16$ inch away from the edge of the fabric.

Edging A narrow decorative border of lace or embroidery trim. It is sewn on top of the raw edge of the fabric and can be used to finish off raw edges of T-shirts and skirts, curtains, etc.

Fabric A cloth used as a covering. It is produced by knitting, weaving, braiding, or felting fibers.

Face A textile term for the right side of the fabric. Sometimes it is difficult to determine which side is the face, so it's helpful when cutting out a project to chalk mark the wrong side of the fabric.

Facing piece A duplicate layer of fabric that is folded back to the inside or outside to keep a raw edge from showing.

Fasteners Snaps or metal hooks and eyes. They come in either black or silver and are available in many sizes. Fasteners are used as hidden closures on skirts, bags, pillows, dresses, and blouses.

Feed dogs These are the pointed metal teeth that rise above the needle plate of a sewing machine, located directly under the presser foot. The feed dogs move the fabric through the machine forward, or backward if you press reverse.

Felled Seam A double-sewn seam that is usually used to sew the side seams of jeans and men's tailored shirts. It creates a clean finish on both sides.

Fold line The exact center of a pattern piece. When folding fabric make sure the fold is parallel to the selvage.

Fold line symbol This appears as a bracket symbol on a pattern, and indicates where a pattern should be placed. Place the fold line along the folded edge of the fabric and pin in place. Don't cut along the fold.

Flounce A kind of ruffle that is made from a circular pattern and attached to a garment as trim.

Fray check A colorless liquid that when applied in small amounts keeps fabric from fraying. It's also better than nail polish to control panty hose runs.

Fuse tape (aka STITCH WITCHERY® and JIFFY FUSE). A tape with glue on both sides that is activated by an iron. Particularly useful for securing fabric layers in place with a crisp finish when stitch marks are undesirable. Available by the yard or in prepackaged strips of varying widths.

Fusible fabric A lightweight nonwoven or tricot (knit) that has glue on one side only. Used inside skirt and pant waistbands, collars, lapels of jackets, or anywhere support or a stiffer finish is needed. If ironed on well, it will survive washing and dry-cleaning.

Grosgrain ribbon A strong, firmly woven ribbon with crosswise ribs. It can be used for decorative trim or as a waistband on a skirt.

Hem The edge of the fabric that is turned in toward the wrong side of a skirt or pant and is sewn in place to finish off the lower edge of a garment. There are many different styles of hem finishes, such as dressmaker finish using hem tape, a sportswear finish using the sewing machine, and a rolled-hem finish using a serger.

Hemline The finished bottom edge on skirts, dresses, jackets, and sleeves.

Hem marker A tool with a ruler and marking powder used to mark the hemline for a skirt.

Interfacing A lightweight fabric that either has glue or does not, which is sewn into garments, bags, and belts to provide support in order to keep it from stretching out of shape.

Join To stitch together pieces of a garment.

Knits Fabrics made by a chain of inter-looping yarns.

Lengthwise grain The warp threads that run up and down the fabric parallel to the selvage, also known as straight grain.

Lockstitch The basic straight stitch formation made by a sewing machine. The top thread forms a loop that locks with the bobbin thread to make each stitch.

Lycra A trademarked name for a man-made fiber, made from a synthetic rubber (spandex). Used as a blend in many knits and woven fabrics to create stretch and better recovery.

Man-made fibers Formerly called synthetic fibers. This term includes all man-made textile fibers that are chemically engineered, such as polyester, acrylic, spandex, nylon, and Lycra.

Nap A surface produced by brushing up the fibers in a cloth. Fabrics with nap will be a different shade of color depending on the direction you cut and sew it together. Fabrics with nap include velvet, corduroy, Ultrasuede, knitted panne, and polar fleece.

Needle A metal spike with a sharp point at one end and an eye to pass thread through at the other end. There are many different types of needles used for sewing. For example, betweens or sharps are used for regular hand sewing; crewel needles with large eyes are for embroidery thread; and beading needles are very thin in order to be able to thread beads. Darners and tapestry needles are used for heavy mending and sewing heavier home decor fabrics. Machine sewing needles range in size. The smaller the number, the finer the needle.

Notions Small supplies used to make a garment such as buttons, snaps, ribbons, thread, etc.

Notches Matching points that are marked on pattern pieces usually in a symbol of a triangle or U. Matching them helps in sewing the garment together correctly.

Overcast stitch A hand stitch that is similar to an overedge stitch. It is used to finish raw seams or for a decorative effect.

Overedge stitch Any stitch used to cover and finish raw seams. Can be done on most home sewing machines using a zigzag stitch.

Overlocker Machines that sew an overlock stitch (see also Serger). Overlockers are four-thread machines. An overlocker will not replace a sewing machine since it cannot do a lockstitch. All overlockers perform the function of trimming, edging, and seaming fabric.

Placket A type of opening in a garment, covering fastenings and zippers or giving access to a pocket.

Parallel Anything that measures an equal distance apart. For example, the straight grain on your pattern piece must be parallel to the selvage.

Pillow form Usually made out of Dacron fiberfill and comes in different sizes for inserting into coverings.

Pins Small pieces of steel with sharp points used to hold fabric together when sewing. They come in many different sizes and varieties. It is best to buy size 17 or 20 for all-purpose use. The nickel-plated stainless steel variety can easily be picked up by a magnet if dropped on the floor. Some pins come with a plastic ball at the top; these are generally used by quilters.

Piping or **Cording** A narrow strip of fabric folded on the bias that sometimes has cording filler in it. It is used to trim a pillow edge or a garment.

Polyester A man-made fiber made from plastic. It resists wrinkles and washes very easily. Many fabrics are blends with polyester.

Presser foot lifter A lever on the back of the sewing machine that raises the presser foot up and down.

Rolled hem A very small hem made on an overlock machine. It also can be made by using a zigzag stitch on a sewing machine or by hand. It is seen on scarves and clothing as an edge finish.

Rotary cutter A cutting tool that must be used with a cutting mat. Great for cutting straight strips of fabric or tougher coverings such as leather.

Seam Where fabrics are joined together by hand sewing or machine sewing.

Seam allowance The distance between the cut edge of the fabric and the sewing line of the seam.

Seam binding A narrow woven tape, resembling ribbon, used to cover the raw edge of a hem. An iron-on seam binding that can be pressed on without sewing is also available.

Seam guide There are several seam guides made, but the best is a magnetic seam guide. It helps you sew straight seams. Place it on the needle plate of the machine at the distance you want from the needle.

Seam line The line that the seam is sewn on.

Selvage The woven or printed edge on each side of the length of a fabric. It won't fray. Sometimes you can identify it by its little poke holes, contrast band, or fringe. Knits don't have this kind of edge; instead there are poked holes and a stiff finish on each long side of a knitted fabric.

Serger (see also Overlocker). This is a five-thread machine that sews an overlock stitch and a chainstitch alongside the overlock stitch.

Sewing machine foot A plastic or metal attachment that holds your fabric under

the needle. There are many different types of sewing feet. Most machines come with extra feet. Refer to the instruction book that comes with your machine as each foot is designed to sew different treatments. For example, a zipper foot is designed so you get closer to the edge. It can be used to sew elastic to a skirt or add piping to a pillow. Of course, it can be used to sew in a zipper also.

Shirr To gather up fabric into a ruffle.

Slit An opening from the hem up on a skirt or dress. Usually seen in a tapered silhouette because it allows you to walk more easily.

Snap fasteners Metal grippers that come in black or silver, available in several sizes. Used to snap close the very top corner of a dress or jacket. Also can be used to close the envelope side of a pillow cover and on baby clothes.

Stitch length The average length setting for most machine sewing is 2.5 or 3 for general sewing and 4 or 5 for machine basting.

Straight grain Same as lengthwise grain. Pattern pieces are pinned to the fabric so the straight grain line printed on the pattern is parallel to the selvage.

Tailor's chalk A small solid piece of chalk used for marking. It can be greasy like a crayon or dry and powdery. The dry clay chalk is best since it doesn't leave a permanent mark.

Tailor's ham A basic tool used when pressing. It is a firm cushion that looks like a canned ham; sometimes also called a dressmaker's ham. Used to shape darts, sleeves, and other places that are a curved shape.

Thimble An aid for efficient hand sewing; it should fit snugly on the middle finger of the needle-holding hand. It aids in pushing the needle through cloth and will take a little getting used to, but really helps with your hand sewing technique.

Tapestry A heavy fabric that is woven in a floral design, story design, or paisley. It is commonly used for bedspreads, upholstery, handbags, pillows, and coats.

Tencel A trademarked name for a new type of cellulose or rayon fiber.

Top-stitch A decorative stitch used on top of the garment. It is usually $1/8$ to $1/4$ inch away from the finished edge of the garment or project.

Thread Very thin twisted fibers or filaments used for sewing. There are many types of thread for many purposes. The most commonly used for all types of sewing projects is an all-purpose thread, which is a cotton-wrapped, polyester core thread.

Tracing paper A waxy paper that is available in different colors. It has a crayon-like finish and is like carbon paper. Used with a tracing wheel to transfer pattern markings such as darts.

Tracing wheel A tool with a handle used to transfer pattern markings to fabric by rolling it over tracing paper.

Tuck A fold or pleat in fabric, usually $1/2$ inch deep.

Twin needle Two needles mounted on one post that insert into the needle clamp of most sewing machines. By using two spools of thread on the machine you can sew a double-needle jean effect on your project. It also makes a professional-looking finish on T-shirts.

Velcro A trademarked name for tape that is used as a fastener. One side is fuzzy and the other side is prickly; when pressed together, they stick.

Viscose A term used in Europe for rayon. Rayon is a cellulose fiber made from wood pulp.

Warp The threads that run vertically or lengthwise in a woven fabric. Warp threads are pulled tight since they need to be strong; they do not stretch.

Weft The threads that run horizontally or crosswise in a woven fabric. Weft threads are not as strong as the warp threads.

Woven A textile structure made by interlacing warp threads with weft threads at right angles. The primary weaves are plain weave, twill, and satin.

Yard A term used to measure 36 inches of running length. Fabric is generally sold in yards.

Yardstick A wooden or metal ruler that is marked at intervals of inches — one yard (or 36 inches) long. Helpful when laying pattern pieces on the straight grain and also can be used to measure hemlines of bias-cut garments by placing the short end on the floor at right angles to the hem.

Yarn An assemblage of fibers or filaments, either natural or man-made, twisted together to form a continuous strand.

Yoke A pattern piece or panel in the top of a jacket, blouse, shirt, or hip area of skirts or a back panel on basic jeans.

Zipper foot A specialty sewing machine foot that is narrow so you can get closer to the edge of a zipper. It can be used also for sewing braiding, piping, and elastic.

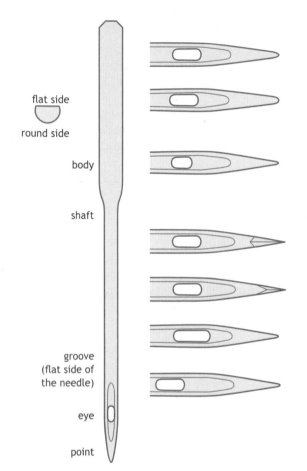

flat side

round side

body

shaft

groove
(flat side of
the needle)

eye

point

Sewing Machine Needle Types

UNIVERSAL needle used for all-purpose sewing on wovens and loose knits.

BALL POINT needle used for sewing knits. Ball point slips between fibers of fabric preventing damage to fabric.

STRETCH needle with special construction for use with knit fabrics to avoid slipped stitches. Use on spandex- and lycra- containing knits.

DENIM needle with triangular point for use with heavy, tightly woven fabrics.

LEATHER needle with wedge point for piercing leather easily.

TOPSTITCH needle with large eye for use with heavier threads.

BASTING needle with high eye for use when long stitches are required.

A general rule to remember when replacing sewing machine needles, is that the flat side of the needle is placed toward the back of the machine.

Metric Conversion Chart

All conversions here relate to the measurements used in this book.

cm centimeters
m   meters

¹/₈ inch	= 0.3 cm	45 inches	= 114 cm
¹/₄ inch	= 0.6 cm	54 inches	= 137 cm
¹/₂ inch	= 1.2 cm	60 inches	= 150 cm
⁵/₈ inch	= 1.6 cm	¹/₄ yard	= 23 cm
³/₄ inch	= 1.8 cm	1 yard	= 90 cm
1 inch	= 2.5 cm	1¹/₂ yard	= 135 cm
18 inches	= 45 cm	2 yards	= 180 cm/1.8 m
22 inches	= 56 cm	3 yards	= 270 cm/2.7 m
31 inches	= 80 cm	6 yards	= 550 cm/5.5 m

inch ruler

cm ruler

Sewing Machine Needle Size Chart

Type of fabric	Size EU/US	Style
WOVENS		
VERY SHEER Lace, Net, Chiffon, Voile	60/8	Universal
SHEER Cotton Lawn, Taffeta, Organdy, Crépe de Chine	70/10	Universal
LIGHTWEIGHT Polyester/Cotton, Gingham	70/10	Universal
LIGHTWEIGHT COAT-SUITING Wool blends	90/14	Universal
MEDIUMWEIGHT Wool, Wool blends, Nylon, Cotton Piqué, Brocade, Velvet, Terrycloth	80/12	Universal
NYLON Outerwear, Ski wear	80/12	Universal
MEDIUM WEIGHT COAT-SUITING Tweeds	100/16	Universal
HEAVY Denim, Corduroy, Sailcloth Duck	90/14	Denim
HEAVYWEIGHT COAT-SUITING Garbardines, Double-faced Wool, Melton Cloth	110/18	Universal
EXTRA HEAVY Canvas, Upholstery, Drapery	100/16 90/14—110/18	Denim Universal
KNITS		
LIGHTWEIGHT Lingerie, Tricot	70/10 75/11	Universal Stetch
MEDIUMWEIGHT Interlock, Swimwear, Jersey, Stretch Terry, Spandex	75/11—90/14	Stretch
HEAVYWEIGHT Double Knit, Velour	80/12—90/14 80/12—90/14 90/14	Universal Ball point Stretch
FAUX FUR Fur-like fabrics	90/14—100/16	Universal
LEATHER		
FAUX LEATHER, SUEDES Ultrasuede®, Sofrina®	75/11	Stretch
UNSUPPORTED VINYLS Polyester/Cotton, Gingham	90/14—100/16	Denim
LIGHT TO MEDIUM WEIGHT Polyester/Cotton, Gingham	90/14—100/16	Leather
SUPPORTED VINYLS Polyester/Cotton, Gingham	90/14	Denim
HEAVY Polyester/Cotton, Gingham	90/14—110/18	Leather

Size Chart for Patterns

Hipster drawstring pants

size (HIP)	inches
Petite	38
Small	40
Medium	44
Large	47
X-Large	50

T-shirt

size (BUST/CHEST)	inches
Petite	36
Small	38
Medium	40
Large	42
X-Large	44

Scarf halter wrap-around dress

size (BUST)	inches
Petite	36
Small	38
Medium	40
Large	42
X-Large	44

ELISSA K. MEYRICH is the pioneer of hip sewing, and founder of SewFastSewEasy, a retail and online business focusing on fashion and home decor sewing.

A longtime garment industry designer, owner of her own sportswear company and former instructor at Parsons School of Design, Elissa is renowned for developing a unique approach to sewing using fashion industry techniques.

She is the author of *SewFastSewEasy: All You Need to Know When You Start to Sew* and *Rip It! How to Deconstruct and Reconstruct the Clothes of Your Dreams*.

Visit the website at:
www.sewfastseweasy.com

DOMINIC HARRIS is a UK-based designer and photographer who has 20 years experience in working to the most demanding of briefs.

Dominic met the author at a New York concert and has worked with her for many years. As a result, he can now run up an outfit in an afternoon when left alone with a sewing machine and some interesting fabrics.

He would like to thank Nahoko Kojima for her invaluable assistance on this project.

See his work at: www.domharris.com